THE ECHOING GREEN

The Echoing Green

MEMORIES OF REGENCY AND VICTORIAN
YOUTH

GILLIAN AVERY

COLLINS

ST JAMES'S PLACE LONDON

Also by Gillian Avery

VICTORIAN PEOPLE
19TH CENTURY CHILDREN
(with Angela Bull, published by Hodder & Stoughton)

Novels

THE WARDEN'S NIECE
TRESPASSERS AT CHARLCOTE
JAMES WITHOUT THOMAS
THE ELEPHANT WAR
TO TAME A SISTER
THE GREATEST GRESHAM
THE PEACOCK HOUSE
THE ITALIAN SPRING
CALL OF THE VALLEY
A LIKELY LAD

First published 1974
© Gillian Avery 1974
ISBN 0 00 192366 8
Set in Monophoto Baskerville
Made and Printed in Great Britain by
William Collins Sons & Co Ltd Glasgow

Contents

Introduction

WHEN I was eight or so I made a birthday card for my mother to accompany my usual offering of a threepenny bunch of violets. Inside was the rather chilling reminder "Time, like an ever-rolling stream, bears all its sons away." We sang that hymn at school on what was then called Armistice Day, 11 November; it was my favourite hymn and I thought the words both moving and appropriate for a birthday.

I still do find them moving, though I have learnt a little since then about what people expect (or do not expect) to find on a birthday card. All my life I seem to have been groping to try to express my feelings (very commonplace of course) about how time and history is made up of the feelings and experiences of millions of people who were once so very much alive and who have disappeared without leaving a ripple on the water. When I first saw Oxford I could hardly bear to walk across a college quadrangle for thinking of all the feet who had hurried there before me, on the same stones, without a thought that they would ever grow old.

To try to give expression to something of this I have assembled the experiences of eighteen people whose childhood or youth fell during the last century. None of them made history in the generally accepted sense of the word, and though three or four of them achieved mild fame in their day I doubt whether any one of them is remembered except by the specialist. But from the memories of their youth we get a glimpse far more vivid than any historian's summary could convey of what it felt like, say, to be afraid of Napoleon invading England; to be poor during the Hungry Forties; to see railways coming into your country village.

There was of course a vast choice of material; the 19th century marks the beginning of the interest in the experiences of childhood, which up till then had been contained, so far as biography went, in a brief, factual summary in a couple of opening paragraphs. I have tried to select memories which cover as wide a range of backgrounds

7

as possible, but which would at the same time, when pieced together, show the enormous change as England moved from the slow, sleepy collection of provinces that Mary Howitt knew in her childhood, to the bustling urban civilization that it had become by 1887.

Care of course has to be used with autobiographies and memoirs. They are usually written sixty or seventy years after the events. You have to allow for hindsight; for adult comments and interpolations getting in the way of what really did happen. I have done my best to prune these and pick out the really illuminating episodes. Alexander Somerville's description of how the boys at his school in the 1820's played, not at cowboys and Indians or cops and robbers, but at ragged radicals and soldiers, is one such, so is Charles Shaw's description of seeing in the flickering candlelight the thin, bare ribs of the frightened workhouse boy who was going to be punished for running away.

I have had to put in a certain amount of explanatory narrative; and to summarize lengthy passages. To modern taste the usual run of Victorian writing is overweighted with words, and the less educated the writer the more words he liked to use. So the shoeblack who described how he was shipwrecked sounds more like a prosy schoolmaster than a boy, and John Shipp who became a soldier at thirteen fills his narrative with very florid poetic flourishes and unconvincing invented dialogue. So from neither of these was I able to quote as much as I would have liked.

A book like this needs some sort of framework, and I have used the writings of Mary and William Howitt. They were modest literary figures in their day, but now, in spite of the bulky writings they left behind, they are very little remembered. They were always better as onlookers and recorders than they were as original writers, and I have drawn lavishly on their memories, not only of their childhood, but the childhood of others. Mary's life usefully takes in two Golden Jubilees – of George III and Queen Victoria, 1809 and 1887, which is roughly the period from which I selected my material. I have stretched it a little at either end, to take in the beginnings of John Shipp's military career which started before Mary was born, and to add as a postscript a chorister's account of Queen Victoria's funeral. (It wavers delightfully between lofty thoughts about her greatness, and glee at the ten shillings the organist gave the choir to spend on sweets.)

I have given almost as much thought to the pictures as to the text,

8

choosing as far as possible from books of the appropriate period. Nobody who has not done picture research (and here I ought to thank Mary Petter who twenty years ago taught me how to set about it) can realize the elation you feel at finding a picture which exactly portrays an episode you have described. The Lord Lieutenant of Ireland's son in his page's costume was a case in point. It was startling to see the boy in the *Illustrated London News* of 1868 just after I had been copying down his description of his excitement, not about the costume, but about the sword that went with it. Besides historical illustration such as this, I have also found pictures from contemporary children's books. In this connection I should like to thank very warmly Miss Joyce Whalley of the Victoria and Albert Museum Library for the most generous help she has given me, and for the notes for her own book that she has put at my disposal.

The greater part of the illustrations were photographed at the Bodleian Library at Oxford. To this library, and to the kindness, courtesy, and patience of the staff, and their readiness to waive formalities, I can never properly express my indebtedness. This time I have drawn heavily on the goodwill, which has never failed, of the staff in the stacks, and in the John Johnson Collection. I do not believe there is a library in the world that can equal Bodley in these qualities, and I am truly grateful to be able to work there.

Oxford, 1973.

GEORGE 3rd from 1760 who has ever set an example of Virtue and Piety.

Long life to the George that we have in his stead.

Prologue

SPANNING THE CENTURIES

"As we next morning left Leicester, the bells of all the churches rang; flags floated here and there from the public buildings and church towers, processions were moving along, and all was astir. 'What is this all about?' we asked. Our mother told us that it was to celebrate what was called a jubilee, because King George III had now reigned fifty years."

Mary Botham was ten years old when she and her sister Anna set out with their mother on 24 October, 1809, from the small town of Uttoxeter in Staffordshire to go to a Quaker boarding school in Surrey. They travelled by chaise; a large, new black leather trunk strapped on outside, one or two smaller ones inside. Surrey was immeasurably far from Staffordshire in Georgian England and the

pre-railway age, and they did not expect to come home for any holidays. It was the first time they had left their home town; travelling, except short distances by the stage wagon which lumbered slowly and ponderously over the rutted roads, was a costly luxury. Even the wealthy did not undertake journeys lightly.

Mary's wondering question, "What is this all about?" shows the seclusion in which it was possible to live in those far-off days, when a child could be ten years old and still be quite cut off from the world.

She was to live to see another jubilee; Queen Victoria's Golden Jubilee, celebrated in June, 1887. Mary was living in Germany then, an old lady, widowed for many years. The tight little world in the middle of England from which she and her husband and their forebears had come had burst asunder, scattering the family all over the globe. Mary and her husband William Howitt spent the last decades of their lives wandering over Switzerland, Germany, and Italy. Their eldest son had settled in Australia, another son had died in New Zealand. One of William's brothers had emigrated to Australia too, and Mary's youngest sister had departed for America many years before.

Mary died in 1888, nearly ninety years old. During those years England had changed more swiftly than perhaps it has ever done. Her life-span did not only link four reigns and two golden jubilees; it linked two epochs, the ages before and after the railways; a countryside divided into close little provinces whose way of life had altered little for centuries had become a new England, the workshop of the world, where the larger part of the population lived in towns.

Mary and her husband William Howitt both came of Quaker stock. Her father's family had lived for generations in Staffordshire; his in Heanor, Derbyshire, only about sixteen miles away. Both of them, before they ever met, had independently decided that they wanted to be writers. They spent their lives at their desks, spinning words. Mary wrote poems, stories for children, tales about provincial life in the past, and undertook translations and any literary work that was offered to her. William, more headstrong and passionate, flung himself into a variety of causes including politics and spiritualism, and wrote about his enthusiasm of the moment. But he also had a deep-rooted love for the countryside, and was at his best when he was recording country scenes and country ways.

The Howitts were never more than minor literary figures, even in their own lifetime, admiring the great ones who held the stage. And they saw so many great ones come and go. Three kings of England died; politicians came to power; governments were overthrown. Pitt was Prime Minister when they were children; the American Constitution was only a few years old; Napoleon was menacing Europe. By the time they reached old age France had long ceased to be an enemy; America had emerged from her own civil war.

Fashions in literature had changed. Byron had been the great hero of their youth. In 1824 when he died it seemed as though the sun was extinguished, and with hundreds of others they filed sorrowfully past his coffin as it rested a night in Nottingham on its way to burial in the church of Hucknall Torkard.

"We laid our hands on the coffin. It was a moment of enthusiastic feeling to me. It seemed to be impossible that the wonderful man lay actually within that coffin. It was more like a dream than the reality."

13

BYRON'S TOMB AT HUCKNALL

And Scott! They saw him at Melrose in 1822. A waiter rushed in while they were breakfasting, exclaiming "'If you want to see Sir Walter Scott, it's he!' We rushed to the window, and beheld the great genius in the North. He was quietly reading a newspaper while the horses were changed." Ten years later Mary wrote to her sister: "Were you not grieved at the death of Sir Walter Scott? Never did there live a man who has so largely contributed to the happiness of his race."

Byron and Scott gone, they turned to Wordsworth. The news of his death in 1850 came to them "like a solemn knell, or the sinking of the sun behind the mountains." Their literary heroes were now younger than themselves. Dickens, Thackeray and Browning were all born when Mary was a child, William a young man.

The Howitts' early married days were spent in the troubled post-Napoleonic period, when England seemed poised on a knife edge, with a gulf of revolution below.

"Those were certainly melancholy times [wrote Mary]. The poor were suffering dreadfully. Labourers in the southern counties toiled like slaves for sixpence [2½p.] a day, and with every spark of independence smothered, from the necessity of receiving parish relief. No wonder, then, at the spirit of insurrection among these poor peasants."

The Radicals were the spectres of those years. People were uncertain who exactly they were or what they might do if roused, and parents frightened their children with threats of them, as Mary and her sister had been frightened by tales of Napoleon and the French. In 1831 William and Mary were living in Nottingham where trade was suffering fearfully from disturbances on the Continent. The people, desperate with want, put all their hopes on the Reform Bill then before Parliament. The Reform Bill, they thought, would make their grievances known and put bread into the mouths of their starving children. From their house in the middle of the town the Howitts could hear the roar of angry crowds of stockingers and lacemakers, and their little daughter Anna Mary would tremble with terror.

When the Lords threw out the Bill, the angry crowds set fire to Nottingham Castle, the property of the Duke of Newcastle who had been among those voting against it. William watched the sight from the roof of the house, first the dense throngs in the vast market place, "their black heads looking like a sea of ink," and then the flames spreading through the castle with "figures as of black demons dancing in the midst of the flames in the upper rooms whilst cries as dread and demoniac were yelled forth from below."

The Nottingham riots left a bitter aftermath. Many of the rioters were hanged publicly, near the Howitts' house. Others were transported. William became drawn into Radical politics and spoke violently against the Church and the established order, but he softened when the young Victoria came to the throne. This was 1837, he was forty-four by then, old enough to be her father, and when he saw her gleaming in satin as she drove to a state banquet he said she looked charming.

The 1840's brought troubles again. There were ugly rumblings from a population maddened by the high price of food and the failure of the Reform Bill, finally passed in 1832, to fill their empty stomachs or give them votes. The talk was of Chartists now. They were the lurking bogeymen whose power the people feared. Penny postage had come into being on 1 January, 1840, but on an envelope addressed to the Howitts from Liverpool, some unknown person scrawled the slogan, "Id. postage is good, cheap bread would be better." In Ireland there was famine; potatoes rotted in the ground, the streets of Liverpool were full of starving Irish, fever-consumed and in rags. They were pouring into America, bringing the fever with them.

There were sad events at home. Mary's youngest sister, Emma, her husband and children emigrated to America; she never saw them again. The Howitts' second son died from a tubercular knee joint. The doctors had wanted to amputate it, but the parents, remembering how Mary's own brother had died after such an operation (those were the days before anaesthetics or antiseptic surgery) had refused. The paper edited by William, *The People's Journal*, aimed at "the general betterment of the working classes", failed. Emma died in distant Cincinnati, and her mother – Mary's mother – a few months later.

Somehow the black shadows of the '40's passed, and suddenly the Howitts, and England too, were out in the sun.

"One brilliant Sunday morning," wrote Mary in her autobiography, "in the spring of 1851, my husband and I, walking down

INTERIOR OF WESTMINSTER ABBEY, DURING THE CORONATION OF VICTORIA I.
THURSDAY, JUNE 28, 1838.

the Fields from Hampstead, with all London lying before us, suddenly saw a wonderful something shining out in the distance like a huge diamond, the true 'mountain of light'. It marked the first Great Exhibition in Hyde Park, a new feature, not only in the fine view, but in the history of the world. We met a humble Londoner evidently on his way to Hampstead Heath. William said to him, 'Turn round and look at the Crystal Palace shining out in the distance.' He did so, and exclaiming 'Oh! thank you, sir; how wonderful!' stood gazing as long as we could see him."

Mary was full of excitement. "Remember that such a meeting of the ends of the earth has never before occurred," she wrote to her sister Anna, trying to convince her of the supreme importance of the occasion. She described the tumult of London in those days: laden wagons dragging goods to the exhibition site in Hyde Park, the streets thronged with bewildered foreigners in strange and outlandish costumes.

The new era of prosperity was interrupted. After nearly forty years of peace, England in 1853 prepared for a war against Russia in which France, the ancient enemy, was to be an ally. On a Surrey common Mary and a host of other spectators chattered and watched the distant, bright-coloured masses of infantry marching and firing against an imaginary enemy in the August sun. Events in 1854 and '55, in a very real Russian winter, must have made this memory a poignant one.

William by then was in Australia. Gold had been discovered there, he was weary of writing, and though he was sixty he was going to try this new life. Taking his two sons, one twenty-two, the other fifteen and radiant with expectation, he departed on one of the new screw steamers. Two years later he was back. They had found no gold, only material for two more books, about Australia this time, and the eldest son had stayed behind to settle permanently. He began writing again – Mary had never stopped. But now he dwelt mostly on the past and the passing. The excitement about the railways and coalpits and the possibilities of steam had waned. He grieved for a rural England that was disappearing. From their house in the hills north of London the Howitts could see, as William wrote

"ever-devouring London, as it crept ever nearer. The rapid advance of this monster of burnt clay along the feet of those smiling hills, east and west, far and wide, comes up as it were a great army to desolate and trample them down. See the front rank of the great house-army far as the eye can reach before you on either hand coming on with a step steady as time and inexorable as death; on every side the tide of population has rolled on with bricks and mortar in its rear."

England was losing its hold upon them, and life was cheaper abroad. In 1870, with their youngest daughter, they left for Switzerland and never returned. In Switzerland they were surrounded by feverish discussion about the progress of the Franco-Prussian war, and there was wild joy in Zurich when news came that the French emperor had surrendered and fled to England. William was enraged by the behaviour of Prussia – who were these arrogant barbarians to devastate a large part of Europe? – and by the mean slavish attitude of countries like England who stood by and made no protest. Nearly eighty years old and full of anger, he wrote a last book denouncing the attackers and the neutrals. But the war over, they could now travel safely to Rome. Here too there was great unrest: the papal states had been seized by the forces of Victor Emmanuel and the pope was a prisoner in the Vatican.

In 1871, the year that Wilhelm I of Prussia was proclaimed emperor of a united Germany, William and Mary celebrated their golden wedding. They picnicked in the country outside Rome, and Mary recalled the wedding day in Uttoxeter.

"Fifty years ago, William and I with our nearest relations, walked to Meeting and all the little town of Uttoxeter looked on. We had some friends to dinner – a better one than usual (if I remember rightly a cook was engaged from the White Hart). Then William and I and all the young people strolled up the garden and up to the Bank Closes; after our return, rain fell. We had more friends to tea – those who had not been invited to dinner. Afterwards the sun came out and we left in quite a splendid sunset. I remember so well how bright it was after the rain, and have often thought it was like our lives and that for us those words might be fulfilled 'At evening time it shall be light'. "

William died in 1879, on the same day and at the same hour as

Is the STATION, with bustle and din,
Where some folks get out, and others get in.

Is the TUNNEL, that's under the ground,
Here the whistle is heard with a very long sound.

Is the URCHIN, so simple and small,
Who cannot make out how the train goes at all.
V is the VIADUCT crossing the road,
Where the river beneath is oft overflowed.

his brother Francis died in Heanor – the town of his birthplace.
When Mary had recovered from the loss, she and her sister Anna
began to piece together material for her autobiography. Anna had
come across a pocket book with locks of hair:

"your hair so bright and lovely, and of dear Charles and Emma such
beautiful curls; and then patterns of silk – a bit of your wedding
dress, a pale grey colour and only think a pattern of that very
sage-green poplin, as we called it, which was our best dresses in
1818 and which I remember our putting on because they were our
prettiest dresses that afternoon when dearest William first came to
Uttoxeter. But I think I am wrong, we did not put on our most
becoming dresses (as we thought) till the second evening we saw
him, because we thought he was so nice he was worth dressing for."

Mary's thoughts dwelt on links with the past.

"Our family dates are of interest. Our great grandfather Wood the
Patentee was born in 1671; Charles II reigned till 1685, therefore
he lived 14 years into the reign of that monarch. Our grandfather
Charles Wood was born in 1702; our mother in 1764; you and I,
now living in 1879, space over as it were 207 years and we are thus
united by two generations (or three if you reckon the Patentee) to
the time of Charles II. I think it very remarkable, and on our father's
side two generations link us to the last Scotch Rebellion; for do you
not remember how our great-uncle James Botham talked about
the army coming to Apsford and how before they came [the Bothams]
buried their plate and how the Scotch Highlanders sliced the big
round cheeses and toasted them before the camp fire using their
claymores for toasting forks and ate it with slices of loaves? In this
way, I think we are two remarkable old women."

She died tranquilly in Rome in 1888, the year that two Emperors
of Germany died, and were succeeded by the grandson of the girl
queen whom middle-aged William had seen driving to the state
banquet in 1837. She could look back to the Napoleonic threat; by
the year of her death the stage was set for a new menace in the
following century – a German one.

Mary

IN THE SHADOW OF
THE FRENCH WARS

"WHEN this lifelong incubus ceased," Mary Howitt wrote of the Napoleonic Wars, "we were freed from a terrible anxiety." England had been at war with France for six years when Mary was born in 1799; she was sixteen when the shadows at last cleared in 1815.

Little as Mary and her sister Anna were aware of the world outside their Staffordshire town, they knew of the war. There was no escaping the talk of it. Betty, the maid who looked after them, had a father who was a tailor, and like other tailors, he was busily making uniforms for the volunteers who were being mustered because of the threat of a French invasion. Betty brought the children pieces of scarlet cloth, and they dressed their dolls as volunteers. Outside, the boys of the town were drilling and exercising and marching about and playing soldiers.

"'Run down to the bottom of the garden and see if the French are not come over the New Bridge!' was the often-repeated ruse of old James Rotherham the joiner, when we bothered him for his tools or were in his way.

"'The French are coming; are really and truly coming!' said James Dumerlo, the half-silly painter, in the wantoness of his mischievous spirit. 'They have burnt Lichfield down to the ground, and have killed all the women and children, and will be here to-night or to-morrow at furthest!' And these threats, though they had proved themselves false so many times, never failed, in conjunction with the gloomy conversation we heard continually from persons whose opinions we respected, to cast an unpleasant damp on our spirit."

But it was their parents' talk that frightened Mary most. When such grave people as these talked so seriously of what should be done if Napoleon came to Uttoxeter then there was indeed something to fear. She would remember the Israelite and Jewish wars in the Old Testament, and shudder to think that this might perhaps happen outside their own door.

"Our parents took little drives in the pleasant summer evenings, mostly one of us children going with them. They talked together of the war, of fearful battles, the increasing price of food, the distress of the poor, the increase of the army, of the jails being filled with young men-friends who were resolutely determined not to serve in the army. The hatred and bitterness against the French that rose in our young hearts I cannot describe. We were frightened out of our wits at the prospect of an invasion; but I remember consoling myself with the thought, when driving through Lord Vernon's park at Sudbury, that at all events those frog-eating French would marvel at such magnificent trees, because they could have nothing like them in their miserable France."

How long would it have been, one wonders, before Uttoxeter would have had the news of an invasion? It lay in the middle of England, remote from neighbouring towns, surrounded by pastures,

woods, and beyond these, moorland. Not even the mail coach called when Mary was a small child. Instead, the letters came by a boy who fetched them daily from a neighbouring town through which the mail passed. He blew a shrill tin horn as he rode into the town. If he brought news of a battle won against the terrible Napoleon he would come galloping in with ribbons streaming from his hat, and quarter of an hour later all the church bells would be ringing. If it was a defeat he would come in at the same speed, but there would be no ribbons, no clamouring bells, and in Uttoxeter the people would be hurrying anxiously into the streets, asking the news.

Mary could remember a day when rejoicing and mourning mingled. It was 26 October, 1805, "a Saturday when the news of the victory of Trafalgar* and the death of Nelson was brought. The bells rang out a merry peal, and then were dropped, and after a pause the muffled notes fell in minute strokes over the hushed streets and people went about grave and sad. It was a dull October day when the news reached us and the drizzling rain added to the sadness."

Then, during those war years, Uttoxeter seethed with an excitement that was not connected with any victory or defeat. The stage-coach was going to call daily, travelling from London to Manchester, via Birmingham. Up till then the poor roads north of Uttoxeter, axle-deep in mud most months of the year, and passable only by pack-

* The battle had been fought on Monday, 21 October.

horses and riders, had contributed to the isolation of the little town. The excitement reached even the Bothams' secluded home, where Mary and Anna were shielded by their Quaker parents from the noise and hubbub of the outside world. The maid who looked after the two children was allowed to take them to see the coach arrive.

It was a great event in the little town, comparable with the stir that a new railway might make a generation later. "I never felt so excited in my life," Mary wrote, "as when it came dashing down the street all covered with ribands, and flags flying, and a French-horn blowing." The changing of the horses was a great sight, too. The new team was there, ready to replace the old. In days to come, when mail-coach service was at the height of its efficiency, changing the teams might be finished in three minutes. When Mary first saw it, it took twenty minutes or more, but this was all the better for the children who watched. They could talk of nothing but coaches that evening, and for many days to come they played at coaches in the

garden, waving strips of red and blue paper, trimmed off the new wallpapers that were being put up in the house, and imitating as well as they could the fanfares of the French horn.

The daily visit of the stage coach was one step towards modern England. The destruction of the Forest of Needwood on the outskirts of the town was another, and for the desolation of this "glorious relic of ancient times, older than the existing institutions of the kingdom, older than English history", as Mary described it, her own father was partly responsible. The Forest of Needwood had been there long before Uttoxeter, a wild, wooded, roadless stretch of country, extending many miles. But by the end of the 18th century the English countryside was being tamed; gradually common land such as this was being divided up, allotted to private owners, and enclosed. Needwood's turn came in 1800, and to Mary's father was given the post of surveyor of its disafforestation. It was a post that he had much wanted, because at that time the family affairs were at a low ebb.

"On the day when any favourable decision ought to arrive by post, my mother, waiting and watching, saw the postboy ride into the town, then, somewhat later, the letter-carrier enter the street, deliver here and there a letter, and pass their door. She did not speak to her husband of a disappointment, which he was doubtless equally experiencing. But after they had both retired to rest, if not to sleep, they heard in the silence of the little outer world, the sound of a horse coming quickly up the street. It stopped at their door. My father's name was shouted . . . He hastened to the window, and was greeted by the words, 'Good news, Mr Botham. I am come from Stafford. I have seen the Act. You and Mr Wyatt are appointed the surveyors.'

. . . "On Christmas Day, 1802, Needwood Chase . . . was disafforested. It was followed by a scene of the most melancholy spoliation. There was a wholesale devastation of the small creatures that had lived for ages amongst its broadly-growing trees, its thickets and underwood. Birds flew bewildered from their nests as the ancient timber fell before the axe; fires destroyed the luxuriant growth of plants and shrubs. . . .

"For upwards of nine years the work of dividing, alloting, and enclosing continued. The rights of common, of pasture, of pannage (feeding swine in the woods), of fuel, and of making birdlime from the vast growth of hollies, claimed by peasants, whose forefathers had built their turf cottages on the waste lands; the rights of more im-

portant inhabitants to venison, game, timber, &c., had to be considered by the Commission of the enclosure, and compensated by allotments of land. On 9 May, 1811, the final award was signed, by which the freeholders' portion was subdivided amongst the various persons who had claims thereon. It was, consequently, a source of deep thankfulness to my father, who had throughout refused gifts from any interested party, that all claimants, from the richest to the poorest, were satisfied with their awards."

Over a period of nine years Mr Botham divided out the area of the devastated forest, creating new roads and farmlands and pleasure grounds. Sometimes he allowed the children to go with him. Their mother would take them to meet him, perhaps to have tea at the house of one of the Forest farmers. Mary and Anna loved the Staffordshire country – "districts of retired farms, where no change came from age to age; tall old hedges surrounding quiet pastures; silent fields, dark woodlands, ancient parks, shaded by grey gnarled oaks and rugged gashed old birch-trees; venerable ruins, shrouded by the dusky yew."

The great excitement when they were small children was the spring visit to the weaver in the next valley to take the yarn their mother had spun and choose the patterns for the cloth.

"Our mother in the winter spun a great deal. It was not the custom for gentlewomen to spin in those midland parts of England at that time; spinning was a fashion which had gone out for a quarter of a

century at least, but she was from South Wales, a woman of strong energetic character, who, adhering to good usage rather than fashion, had brought the wheel with her, and used it for some years after her marriage. She spun, therefore, every winter, many pounds of flax into beautifully fine yarn, which used to hang in hanks, as they were finished, at the top of the kitchen, among hams, salted beef, and dried herbs. I have now table-linen of her spinning, and most probably shall leave some of it to my own children. She was an excellent spinner, and it used to be the delight of us children to sit beside her, and lay by turns our heads upon her knee, which were thus, as we thought, agreeably rocked, or rather trotted, by the turning of the wheel, whilst she repeated to us long portions of Thomson's Seasons, of which she was extremely fond, Gray's Elegy, passages from Cowper, and other long poems, all of a meditative and serious character. I can recall now the sound of her voice, mingled with the busy humming of the wheel, and it seems delightful."

Then, in April or early May, after a week or two of excited antici-pation, came the great day of the expedition to Master Pedley. It was a pleasant walk, even though it was along the turnpike road. The fields were full of flowers, the hedges green with young leaves; there were lambs and goslings, and ducklings on the ponds. And at

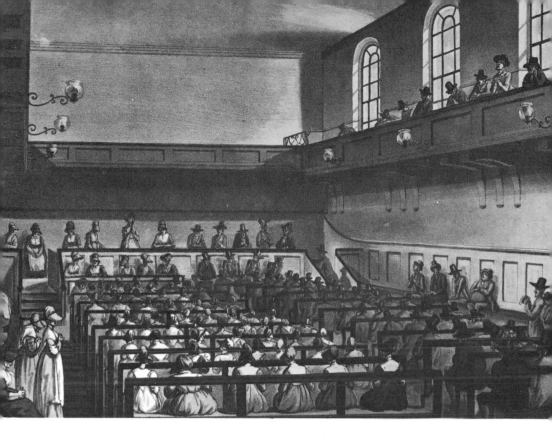

Master Pedley's the old people would be waiting for them, and seemed to know that they would be coming. First the children would go out in the fields to gather cowslips and wild daffodils. "When we returned to the house, we always found the little round stand set out, and the bottle of cowslip-wine, and the seed cake, and gingerbread ready, 'for,' said the old woman, 'I've been a-looking for you these two or three days!' It was a charming thing, this going to Master Pedley's, and, perhaps what made us think most of it, was that it only came once a year."

Few diversions broke the quietness of the Bothams' household. Mary and Anna played for the most part by themselves; Emma, the next child, was not born until Mary was seven, and Charles, the youngest, two years later. The sisters had lessons with their mother, and occupied themselves in a bare upstairs room of the Queen Anne house which had been in the Botham family for generations. Behind lay a long garden, then a brook, and a high ridge fringed with oaks and old thorn trees. In front was the Quaker meeting-house. Here the children were taken to Meeting twice every First Day, as

Sundays were styled in the Quaker fashion. But as it was their father's belief that the soul should be guided by the Inner Light alone, not by human instruction, the girls were given no religious teaching at all, and would sit, uncomprehending, through the long hours of Meeting which often passed in total silence. Mary used to while away the time by fancying imaginary pictures in the blotches of damp on the walls, and in the knobs of the worn wood of the seats.

As might be expected, there were few books. The children were given *The Castle of Instruction*, *The Hill of Learning*, *The Rational Dame*, which seemed, Mary recalled "written on purpose to deter children from reading," though the outside was very pretty, bound in coloured paper, and stamped and printed in green and gold and red. But if they did not have books, they had Nanny Woodings, the maid who looked after them. In front of the parents Nanny was staid and quiet. To the children she was a quite different person. She could imitate animals, she could tell ghost stories and fairy stories which she seemed to believe in herself. She pointed out houses where murders and terrible deeds had been done, she sang them ballads from halfpenny sheets bought at fairs, and taught them whist which they played on a teatray on her knee. The children were sworn to secrecy about such things. One of their favourite stories was how Nanny and her sister had as children been frightened out of their wits by a couple of "canal navigators", the predecessors of the railway navvies whose lawless violence was to terrify country people when the railways were being built. The two little girls had been taking ducks to market when they met the "canal navigators", had fled, and had been rescued by a gentleman who took them back to a palace of a house "which looked grander even than the Cathedral at Lichfield."

But it was the stories of Rhoda, the girl who looked after them while Nanny was busy with the new babies, that got them into serious trouble. She was a gossip and chatterer. She used to horrify them with stories of the bull-baiting in Uttoxeter, how the dogs were ripped up, the pools of blood in the streets, the death of the bull after it had been savaged for three days. She spoke about secret meetings with lovers, and love letters, and at Rhoda's dictation the nine-year-old Mary wrote one herself which she put for safe-keeping into one of her father's devotional books. Samuel Botham found the letter that Sunday before he went to Meeting and Mary was summoned to her parents. "I suppose I felt something as our first parents did

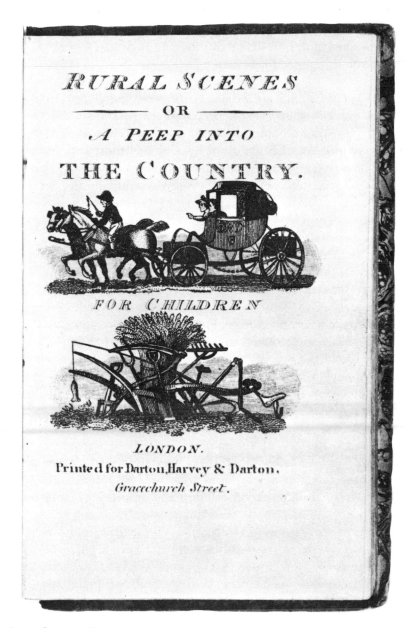

RURAL SCENES

— OR —

A PEEP INTO

THE COUNTRY.

FOR CHILDREN

LONDON.

Printed for Darton,Harvey & Darton,

Gracechurch Street.

when God called them in the Garden," she said, recalling that dreadful moment. A close friend advised that the girls should not be left with servants, and that they should go to school.

So Mary and Anna went first to a day school in Uttoxeter, then, when that closed, they made the long journey to Croydon to a

Friends' school, through a countryside that had momentarily forgotten about the war, and was rejoicing because George III had been on the throne for fifty years.*

"Throughout all the day we saw nothing but festivity; at first oxen or sheep carried in procession prepared for roasting whole; great fires burning up, and spits of a gigantic size ready to receive the equally gigantic roast. Processions bearing garlands, and decorated with ribbons, were parading the streets of town or village; bands of music were playing; bells were ringing; public-houses were all astir; schools of children, girls and boys, and town corporations were marching to church; gentlemen's carriages were driving about; country people were jogging along the roads by cartfuls . . .

"A little further on, and people were all coming out of church; corporations, volunteer regiments, schools, clubs, both male and female; gentlemen and ladies, poor folks, old and young, all in their best attire. Then we came to where people were dining, and all was bustle and clamour and clatter. Here sate the town paupers all at a dinner of roast-beef; bread in huge pieces was handed about in clothes-baskets; ale was drawn out of big barrels into foaming cans, and thin hands, whose lank wrists seemed lost in the sleeves of their grey woollen jackets, lifted up the welcome can. But poor people and workhouse paupers were not so much to be pitied then as nowadays. And on that day, apparently, nobody was to be pitied; there was not even a beggar that day in the roads. . . .

"On we went; and now other tables were standing on other greens and in other market-places, and hundreds of women and little children were drinking tea, and ladies and gentlemen, handsomely dressed, were walking about, and the bells were ringing still.

"And now we drove into Dunstable in a blaze of light that made us wild with joy; the town was illuminated; the inn to which we drove was like an enchanted palace; every window was a blaze of light; illuminated crowns, and stars, and great G.R.'s covered the front, mingled with laurels and flags; music pealed from the house, and all was bustle and gaiety. Carriages were driving up; carriages were driving away; and we in our quiet chaise, with our little black

* The jubilee in fact was celebrated at the opening of the fiftieth year of his reign instead of at the close of it as his health was precarious. In 1809 he had a temporary respite from his attacks of insanity.

Warren-Bulkeley-arms, Stockport, Oct. 11, 1809.

At a MEETING,

Held in consequence of a REQUISITION addressed to JESSE HOWARD, Esq., Mayor, for the purpose of determining on the proper means of celebrating the

Fiftieth Anniversary

OF

His Majesty's Accession to the Throne,

ON THE 25th INSTANT,

R. GEE, Esq. in the Chair,

IT IS RESOLVED,

THAT, as it would be highly commendable and decorous in the subjects of so good a King to offer up thanksgivings for the favors which God has been pleased to continue to this country for half a century, by permitting a mild, equitable, and virtuous Sovereign so long to reign; as well as to inculcate a dependence upon Providence, and benevolence towards our fellow-creatures upon so happy an occasion, it be recommended to the Clergymen to perform Divine Service on that day in their respective Churches and Chapels, and to allow Collections to be made therein for the establishment of a fund, to be applied by a Committee, in obtaining, as far as practicable, the liberation from Gaol of such poor Debtors from Stockport, and the places subscribing, as may be found proper objects.

That the Gentlemen of the Town and Neighbourhood do attend at this house, at ten o'clock in the forenoon of the 25th instant, to walk in procession to St. Mary's Church.

That the afternoon be spent in General Rejoicing by all ranks and descriptions of persons; that a large Bon-fire be made in the centre of the Market-place, at which SHEEP or an Ox shall be roasted and distributed, with moderate portions of liquor, to the populace; and that FIRE-WORKS be displayed at night.

That Subscriptions be collected throughout the town and neighbourhood for defraying the expences, and towards the fund for benevolent purposes.

That there be a BALL on the 26th instant at the *Warren-Bulkeley-arms Inn*, under the management of Stewards, to be appointed by the Committee.

That a Committee consisting of twelve Gentlemen be appointed to carry into effect the above Resolutions.

That the Committee do meet at this house at six o'clock this evening.

The Committee accordingly met, and appointed Managers, Stewards and Collectors, and adjourned to Monday the 16th instant, at six o'clock in the evening.

DEANS, PRINTERS, STOCKPORT.

leather trunk strapped behind, ran the risk of being quite over-looked. . . .

"The next day we reached London. London! The very name thrilled us but to speak it. But London did not look half as gay as Dunstable had done. The streets of London through which we drove only bore token of the things that had been. The extinguished lamps which had formed crowns and stars, and great G.R.'s, were then dim and unattractive, like the ashes of a fire which has gone out. We could just get an idea of what had been; it was like looking at a piece of tapestry on the wrong side."

Croydon, now all concrete and bricks and swallowed up by London, was then a quiet little town of one street. Beyond it were nursery gardens, fields of lavender, open commons, pleasant lanes and hills. The school was a small one of ten or twelve children, all the daughters of Quakers, but Quakers of a far less austere habit than Samuel Botham. To these girls Mary and Anna seemed to have come from the uttermost ends of the earth; their name was odd, Uttoxeter seemed unpronounceable, their clothes were peculiar, and their Midland accent quite extraordinary.

At first they sat apart and cried themselves to sleep, but soon they became accepted; Mary was quick at lessons, Anna could skip and play "burnball". They were happy at Croydon, but miserably conscious of the difference between themselves and the others. At Christmas, for instance, everybody went home for the holidays, chattering about Christmas festivities, even though they were Quakers. In the Botham household Christmas Day had always been spent as any ordinary day, and the only communication they received from home that Christmas was a parcel containing six shirts to make up, and a small quantity of dried lemon-peel.

And their clothes, they were indeed mortifying. Certainly all the girls wore plain, Quaker dresses, but Mary and Anna's were peculiarly severe and ugly, and throughout their girlhood were to give them much grief. Samuel Botham's rule in life was self-denial, one which he also imposed upon his family. Anna accepted it (though she wept in secret when he destroyed one of her flower paintings saying it was "better not to indulge in colour", but Mary rebelled against the gloom of his religious feelings. Later she was to give up Quaker practices, and at the end of her life she was received into the Roman Catholic Church.

They were happy, however, at the Surrey school, and sorry when next year they had to leave because of their mother's serious illness. They had one more brief period at school, in Sheffield this time, and then they returned to Uttoxeter to read and study by themselves. On a visit to cousins near Leicester, Mary complained of the dullness of the young men of Uttoxeter; all the young Friends there were so stupid. Cousin Anne Ellis contradicted her. There were many talented and interesting young men in the Society of Friends. But none of them could equal William Howitt, "a real genius and so agreeable."

Four more years passed, and then on 16 April, 1821, William Howitt of Heanor, Derbyshire, married Mary Botham in the Uttoxeter meeting-house, opposite her home.

John

THE LITTLE FIFE-MAJOR

"ONE autumn's morning, in the year 1797, while I was playing marbles in Love Lane and was in the act of having a shot at the whole ring with my blood-alley, the shrill notes of a fife, and the hollow sound of a distant drum, struck on my active ear. I stopped my shot, bagged my marbles, and scampered off to see the soldiers."

If we reckon by this date, John Shipp was twelve years old that year when a recruiting party marched into the small Suffolk market town of Saxmundham, trying to raise troops for the French Wars. He became rather confused about the dates when he came to write his memoirs, and some of them contradict each other, but the main facts are clear; he was an orphan, a soldier's child, brought up in the parish poor-house, and he had the good luck to satisfy a burning ambition (which not many poor-house inhabitants were likely to do) at a remarkably early age.

The speech that the recruiting sergeant delivered to the gaping locals in Saxmundham set young John on fire. "I adjusted my hat

38

with a knowing air, elevated my beardless chin with as much consequence as I could assume, and, raising myself on tiptoe, to appear as tall as possible, I strutted up to the sergeant, and asked him if he would "take I for a sodger"?

But in that year his majesty's government was not recruiting twelve-year-olds, and John had to go back to the poor-house and drill any boy willing to take his orders. "Even the old women in the parish could not pass me without a military salute, such as 'Heads up, missis!' 'Eyes right, missis!' 'Keep the step, missis!'"

And then, one bitterly cold December day he heard the music again. He had been apprenticed to a farmer, and a particularly brutal one, and he was standing in a turnip field with his fingers in his mouth, trying to warm them, and there was the music, coming towards him. When the soldiers passed he was standing at attention giving them a military salute, with the wrong hand, but with fervent enthusiasm. And with fervent enthusiasm he followed them, all the way to Beccles, sixteen miles away.

But it was no good, they still would not take him. The commanding officer was kind; he was given a meal and a few shillings, and sent home in the charge of a sergeant, with a message to the farmer that

THE FARMER'S BOY.

he should be let off punishment. The farmer duly made his promise –
which he kept till next morning, when he "seized me by the neck, and
dragged my clothes off my back. He had with him a double-handed
whip, such as is used by colliers, and with this he lashed me so
unmercifully, that, had not a man, who was labouring in an adjoining field, interfered, he would have killed me."

And so matters went on until the next year. By that time the
government had changed its mind about recruiting twelve-year-olds.
In fact it decided to open the ranks of the army to ten-year-olds, and
form three experimental regiments from boys of ten to sixteen taken
from poor-houses – thus augmenting its forces and relieving parishes
of some of their paupers at one astute stroke.

John Shipp heard the news from one of the parish officers while
he was working in the fields, and instantly threw down his shovel and
marched off with him. From parish funds he was fitted out in new
leather breeches, a coat, a hat and new shoes, and dispatched to
Colchester. The army removed his new clothes (he was allowed to
sell them and raised the sum of £1 1s. 6d. – £1·07½), and put him
into red jacket, red waistcoat, red pantaloons and red forage cap.
They also removed most of his hair, after which the rest of it was tied
back army fashion.

"A large piece of candle-grease was applied, first to the sides of my
head, then to the hind long hair; after this, the same operation was

performed with nasty stinking soap – sometimes the man who was dressing me applying his knuckles instead of the soap. After this operation, I had to go through one of a more serious nature. A large pad, or bag filled with sand, was poked into the back of my head, round which the hair was gathered tight, and the whole tied round with a leather thong. When I was dressed for parade, I could scarcely get my eyelids to perform their office; the skin of my eyes and face was drawn so tight by the plug that was stuck in the back of my head, that I could not shut my eyes; add to this, an enormous high stock was poked under my chin; so that I felt as stiff as if I had swallowed a ramrod, or a sergeant's halberd. Shortly after dinner was served; but my poor jaws refused to act on the offensive, and when I made an attempt to eat, my pad behind went up and down like a sledge-hammer."

He was then put into the band and taught to play the flute, the triangles and the fife. "I was soon made fife-major – no small office, I assure you. I wore two stripes and a tremendous long sash, which almost touched the ground." He strutted around with a cane, and on ceremonial occasions carried a seven-foot silver-headed stick in front of the band, astonishing the spectators "with my double demi-semi twist." He grew out of his red coat, and was given a splendid white silver-laced jacket with two silver epaulettes – his great pride, he was never tired of seeing them flutter in the breeze. The new life was a great improvement on the old; he was a favourite with the officers, though not so much with the other boys.

"I diverted myself with filling the pipes of my comrades with gunpowder; putting a lighted candle in their hands while asleep, then tickling their noses with a straw; tying their great toes together, then crying out fire; blacking their hands with soot, then tickling their ears and noses, to induce them to scratch themselves, and thus to black their faces all over; putting lighted paper between their toes when asleep; pulling the stools from behind them, when in the act of sitting down; sewing their shirts to their bedding when asleep; all these were my constant delight and practice. They led me into many a fight, but that did not discourage me."

The threat of flogging (and this meant the cat-o'-nine-tails with the victim tied to a triangle, military style) and of solitary, dark,

confinement did not discourage him from other offences. He and his
friends stole a goose and hid it in a drum while they were searched
for the booty. They might have got away with it if the goose's death
groans had not been heard. The goose's owner begged them off their
flogging that time, but there was nobody to intercede when young
John "ate his boots." He had been issued with new shoes, but met
"the plum-pudding woman on the way back. Savoury smells came
from her basket, haggling followed, and John left her with a shilling
in his pocket, a quarter of a yard of pudding, and no shoes. He was
ordered seven days imprisonment in the black hole for this. His
spirits rather sank when the heavy door clanged behind the sergeant
and he was left in pitch dark and icy cold, but they soon revived and
he did handstands and somersaults to keep himself warm.

The punishment he most minded was given for his antics with the
fife-major's silver stick. He swaggered and capered so much on one
occasion that he was reduced to the ranks and confined to barracks.
He had the audacity to take his name off the list himself, "for which

Going on board the "Hector" of 74 Guns, lying in Portsmouth Harbour.

I had the felicity of attending drill three times a-day, with my musket reversed and my coat turned inside out." The drill sergeant bullied and whipped him; but he could have endured all this, it was the shame of the turned coat that rankled.

The regiment was not sent to the French wars. They were first dispatched to Guernsey. The small sloop ran into a terrifying storm on the way; at least, John Shipp chose to remember it as such when he described it in the memoirs and set down some dramatic dialogue between the captain and the officers. Apparently a French ship was seen, but luckily made off without a fight, for there was not even a drummer or a bugler to call the soldiers to arms; they were all prostrated with sea-sickness. When they reached land at last, John found that soaked and exhausted and sick though he might be – "I looked like a squeezed lemon, or the bag of a Scotch pipe" – he was still expected to lead the fife band smartly through the town.

They did not stay long in Guernsey; they were ordered back to Portsmouth to prepare themselves for embarkation for South Africa. They were being sent to the Cape of Good Hope to protect the settlers against what John Shipp called "the Caffres", or the Kaffirs as they would now be styled.

He was used to hardship, but the voyage out appalled even him. His ship, the *Surat Castle*, a 1500 ton ship, was grossly overcrowded,

43

Middle-Deck of

"men literally slept on top of one another, and in the orlop-deck*
the standing beds were three tiers high, besides those slinging". If a
boy brought up in a workhouse and a barracks thought that the
living conditions were fearful, they must have been bad indeed.

There was disease even before the voyage started, brought by an
immense number of Lascars† who had been living in England in
abject want and distress, and who were brought on board covered
with sores and vermin, many of them dying. Soldiers, women and
children were all herded and packed in together. The stench between
decks, said John Shipp, was beyond description. Storms added to
the distress; disease spread, and the dead and the dying lay in a
welter of paint, spilt from barrels which had got loose from their
lashings and thundered and rolled over the deck, too heavy for
anybody to secure them.

Then came scurvy, which scarcely anybody escaped. They
staggered round, with monstrously swollen legs, and gums pro-

* The lowest deck.   † East Indian sailors.

...tor", Man of War.

truding beyond the lips, the dying burying the dead. "The sea-gulls soared over the ship, and huge sharks hovered round it, watching for their prey. These creatures are sure indications of ships having some pestilential disease on board, and they have been known to follow a vessel so circumstanced to the most distant clime." John Shipp's legs were as big as drums, his gums enormously swollen, his tongue too big for his mouth, and all he could eat was raw potatoes and vinegar.

But his spirits recovered when they saw land and he "jumped and danced about like a merry-andrew". A fortnight's convalescence for the whole regiment followed, during which there was no enemy more serious than a troop of baboons, who annoyed them so much by thieving that armed guards had to be left to protect their property. Blankets, great coats, anything portable was taken, and the baboons hurled stones at anybody who tried to stop them. "One old grey-headed one who often visited the barracks and was known by the name of Father Murphy, was seen distributing his orders, and planning the attack, with the judgement of one of our best generals." However, Father Murphy was caught one morning in the very act of

45

stealing a sergeant's regimental coat. They felt scruples about killing him, muzzled him instead, and shaved his head and face. "To this ceremony, strange to say, he submitted very quietly, and, when shaved, he was really an extremely good-looking fellow; and I have seen many a 'blood' in Bond Street not half so prepossessing in his appearance." The other baboons treated him as an outcast, and Father Murphy came back to the barracks for protection, and became tame and domesticated.

All this was a diversion, of course, and they soon had to turn to more serious matters. The Kaffirs had risen against the Dutch settlers and were plundering the farms and murdering their inhabitants. It was a guerilla type of warfare, and one that the English troops were quite unused to. The military authorities showed more sense and imagination than usual, and scarlet tunics were replaced with green ones and muskets painted brown so that the soldiers would not show up when they hunted the Kaffirs through the woods where they took refuge.

The Kaffirs were a terrifying enemy. Muskets were no match for their darts, hurled from the cover of woods with unnerving accuracy, and musket balls bounced off the skins that they wore. "Under the garb of night they crawl on their hands and knees, imitating the cries of any animal of the woods, or any bird of the air. At the smallest noise they will lie flat on the ground, so that you may walk close by, and not observe them. . . . It was no unusual thing in the morning to see their spears lodged in the top of our waggons, and close by where we kept watch." The English fought their way through almost impenetrable woods, over tremendous hills and through rivers, all the time harassed by an enemy who was mostly unseen. Their clothes turned to rags, their shoes were replaced by raw buffalo hide. John Shipp had grown six inches during the two years he was out there; his jacket was so tight he could hardly raise his hand to his head, and his trousers now came just over his knees.

He had grown up in other ways too – he had fallen in love. The girl was called Sabina; she was fifteen, he was sixteen, and they met while he was escorting her family, who were Dutch settlers, down to Cape Town. Her father, said John Shipp, was a very gross man, but she was a jewel. For a few delicious days they lived in the present and made no plans for the future, but as Cape Town came in sight John Shipp came back to reality. He and the regiment had been ordered to India: "marriage would not have been consented to by my com-

manding officer, on account of my extreme youth; the thought of any less honourable proposal I could not encourage for a moment; and it soon became clear to me, that there was but one road of escape from the heart-rending necessity of parting at once, and for ever, from my lovely brunette – desertion."

Desertion from the army was a terrible crime, with terrible consequences, but Sabina's tears and pleadings won him over. First he insisted on delivering the officers' baggage which he had brought with him on the overland journey to Cape Town; then, after a great struggle with himself – for he was a devoted soldier – he stole out of the barracks and met Sabina and her family outside the town. They had gone about thirty miles from Cape Town when the provost-marshal thrust his head and a pistol into the waggon and said that if he attempted to move he would be shot. Ten minutes later he was on his way back to the barracks.

He was court-martialled and sentenced to receive 999 lashes, "being more than 50 lashes for every year I was old." But his commanding officer was a kind man who had taken an interest in him since the day he had joined the regiment. He sent for him and told him of the seriousness of the offence, said that he had been deluded by the Dutchman and his family, and dismissed him, forgiven.

He never saw Sabina again. A few weeks later he was in India, and there he applied himself diligently to bettering himself. One of the officers undertook to help him with his reading and writing; he was promoted from drummer-boy to private, then to a corporal, and six months later to a pay-sergeant. Then for his bravery during the siege of Bhurtpore he was given a commission in 1805. From work-house boy to commissioned officer was a most remarkable career in those days of privilege, but John Shipp did it twice. He sold out in 1808 to pay his debts, enlisted again as a private soldier and was again commissioned. In 1823 he left the army for ever; he had criticized his superior officers, and this was not to be tolerated. He spent the last eleven years of his life in surroundings which must have been familiar, in Liverpool workhouse, but this time as its master.

STANDS FOR KAFFIRLAND, CAPE OF GOOD HOPE,
WITH THE NATIVES OF WHICH WE'VE OFT HAD TO COPE;
AND HERE IS A GROUP OF THEM, CRUEL AND FIERCE,
WITH ARROWS ALL POISONED AND SPEARS THAT WILL PIERCE.

PRILLISK THE BIRTHPLACE OF WM CARLTON

William Carleton

THE POOR IRISH SCHOLAR

Not all George III's subjects were anxious for the English to win those wars that overshadowed the Howitts' childhood. In Ireland young William Carleton watched his elders lingering at the cross-roads talking before Mass, and their hope, he said, was that Napoleon would conquer England and come and rule Ireland. "Merciful God!" he wrote in his autobiography. "In what a frightful condition was [the North of Ireland] at that time. It was then, indeed the seat of Orange ascendancy and irresponsible power. . . . There was then no law *against* an Orangeman, and no law *for* a Papist."

He lived in County Tyrone, in a part of Ireland where the Protestant ascendancy was particularly strong. He remembered how in those war years there were corps of volunteers raised against the French threat, "but I never knew of a Roman Catholic to be

49

admitted, with one exception," – the exception was in fact a cousin of his own. These volunteers were in the habit of putting on their uniform and getting their guns and bayonets, and going out at night to search Catholic houses under the pretence of searching for firearms. It happened at his own house, when he was ten, and what made it so bitter to remember was that not only was his father one of the quietest and most respected men in the parish who took no part whatsoever in politics, but that there were friends and neighbours in the search party.

"One night, about two or three o'clock, in the middle of winter, a violent bellowing took place at our door, and loud voices were heard outside. My father got up, alarmed, and asked who was there.

'Open the door, you rebellious old dog, or we will smash it in.'

'Give me time to get on my clothes,' replied my father.

'Not a minute, you old rebel; you want to hide your arms – open, or we smash the door,' and the door was struck violently with the butts of guns. My father, having hurried on his small clothes, and lit a candle, opened the door, when in an instant the house was filled with armed yeomen in their uniform.

'Come, you traitorous old scoundrel, deliver up your damned rebelly gun.'

'My good friends,' replied my father, 'I have no gun.'

'It's a lie, you rebel, it's well known you have a gun. Produce it, or I put the contents of this through you.' And as he spoke the man cocked and deliberately aimed the gun at my father. When my mother saw my father covered by the ruffian's gun, she placed herself with a shawl about her between them, and corroborated what my father said, that we had no gun. She was called a liar; it was notorious we had a gun. In the meantime, some others of them began to institute a search. Two of them went into my sister's bedroom, a third man holding the candle.

'Who is this?' said one scoundrel.

'It's my daughter,' replied my mother, trembling and in tears.

'Well,' he returned, 'let her get up until we have a look at her; it's likely she has the gun in the bed; at all events we'll rouse her a bit – ' and as he spoke, he put the point of the bayonet to her, which he pressed until she screamed with pain. At this moment his companion pulled him back with something of indignant violence, exclaiming:

'Damn your soul, you cowardly scoundrel, why do you do that?'

At this moment my mother, with the ready recollection and presence of mind of her sex, exclaimed:

'I think it likely that all this trouble has come from the little tin gun that Sam Nelson gave the children – here it is,' she proceeded – 'here is the only gun that ever was under the roof. If it's treason to keep *that*, we are rebels' – and as she spoke she handed them the gun. They looked at it, and after some ruffianly grumbling they retired. My sister was slightly wounded in the side."

There was no one in that search party, said William Carleton, who did not know his family intimately. The Sam Nelson who had given the children the toy cannon was a neighbour, and Sam's brother was one of the intruders and never once spoke up for the Carletons.

The Roman Catholics had their own way of avenging themselves against the Protestants; they banded themselves in a nation-wide secret society. Ribbonmen they called themselves, and there was hardly a Catholic boy who could escape becoming one. William himself was drawn into it when he was still a schoolboy, and had sworn the oath before he realized what he had done. When he had kissed the prayer book and gone through the rigmarole the red-headed Hugh Roe McCahy, who had taken him off from a wedding dance to initiate him, told him what Ribbonism meant. It seemed that the whole Catholic population, with the exception of the oldest

51

men, took part in this Ribbonism. If a young man refused to join, he would probably be set upon and beaten up. There was a long oath whose ten different promises swore loyalty to the cause, and there was also the "Words" and the "Grip".

The "Words" were as follows: "What age are we in?" "The end of the fifth." "What's the hour?" "Very near the right one." "Isn't it come yet?" "The hour is come, but not the man." "When will he come?" "He is within sight." The "Grip" was, when shaking hands, to press the point of the thumb on the second joint of the forefinger, and if the person with whom you shook hands was a brother, he was to press upon the middle joint of your little finger.

It was Saturday night that he was sworn in as a Ribbonman, and when he walked to school on Monday, a friend, Frank McGough, came up and asked him "What age are we in?" It was then that he realized that there was hardly a schoolboy or a schoolmaster who was not a Ribbonman.

The battles between Ribbonmen and Orangemen were fearful. In a short story he described one that he had seen when he was fourteen. Both sides had called on men from all the surrounding counties for support, and three to four thousand were involved. It happened at the Lammas fair at Clogher, and the day that it happened was known ever afterwards as "The Day of the Great Fight."

More terrible still was the affair of Wildgoose Lodge, another episode that he described in a short story. "Like many another black national crime," he wrote in his autobiography, "this one resulted from Ribbonism. The members of that accursed Ribbon Society, instead of confining themselves to those objects for which it seems to have been originally designed – a union of Irishmen against their Protestant enemies, and the penal enactments which oppressed them at the time – departed from their original object, and employed its murderous machinery in the following up of private and personal feuds, and enmities amongst themselves."

There was a family called Lynch who lived at Wildgoose Lodge. They were very pious, peaceful and industrious, and they held themselves aloof from Ribbonism, though they were often urged to join it. Then one night they had a visit from members of the society, who smashed in the door and beat them up. When the Lynches recovered they took legal action against the Ribbonmen who had injured them, and the Society swore revenge.

The revenge was planned by a man called Devaun, the parish
schoolmaster and parish clerk. He served mass every Sunday, and
was thought to be beyond suspicion. He summoned his followers to
the chapel, primed them with whiskey, and made them swear on
the altar to follow him blindly and do as they were ordered. Then
they all marched to Wildgoose Lodge and set it on fire. The Lynches
as they appeared at the windows screaming for help were pushed
back into the flames – it is all horribly described in the story, *Wild-*

goose Lodge. Devaun would not let his men leave the spot until the house lay in a pile of ashes.

William Carleton saw for himself the gibbets where the murderers were hanged, though he did not recognize what they were at first.

"One day I went on, guided by the turnings of the way, until I reached a cross-road in a small village, where I perceived a number of soldiers, standing and chatting to each other, and passing their time as best they could. I looked on before me when I had reached this queer little place, and perceived something like a tar sack dangling from a high beam of wood, or rather from the arm which projected from it. There was a slight but agreeable breeze, the sack kept gently swinging backward and forward in obedience to the wind, and I could perceive long ropes of slime shining in the light, and dangling from the bottom.

I was very much astonished, and applied to the soldiers who were near me.

'Pray,' said I, 'what is the nature or meaning of that object which I see up the road there?'

'Why,' said one of them, the sergeant, 'is it possible you don't know?'

'I certainly do not,' I replied, 'nor can I guess what it means.'

'Well, sir,' said he, 'that object is a gibbet – and what you see swinging from it in the pitched sack is the body of a murderer named Devaun; Paddy Devaun swings there – and it's just where he ought to swing.' "

All round the county stood the gibbets, set up near the homes of the hanged men. Every sack was covered with flies, and fruit that autumn was avoided, as something that could not possibly be eaten.

How William Carleton extricated himself from Ribbonism he did not say. Political feuds did not interest him, he was concerned in getting himself an education. Most of his unfinished autobiography is taken up by his accounts of his schools, first the ones he learnt in, then his efforts to find one where he could teach. He was the youngest of fourteen children, though six of them had died before he was born. Neither of his parents had had much in the way of schooling, but his father could repeat most of the Old and New Testament by heart, and was full of legends and stories, old customs and superstitions. His mother sang exquisitely, especially the old Irish songs.

There was nobody who could give the Irish cry, or *keen*, so beautifully, and when she 'raised the keen', as it was called, over the body of a dead relation or neighbour, all the noisy grief of the onlookers was silenced as they listened.

The Carleton parents were very anxious that young William should have an education; schools however were not easy to find in those days. Under the code of William III Catholic education had been outlawed in Ireland, and Catholic schoolmasters were imprisoned and fined. By the beginning of the 19th century these laws were no longer enforced, but the term "hedge school" had stuck – dating from the time when clusters of Catholic children and their masters had crouched in the shelter of a ditch or a hedge, with one pupil on sentry duty to warn of the approach of strangers. The hedge schools of the 1800's were set up in a cabin or a barn by anybody who thought he had the qualifications, and could persuade the farmers and the cottagers to send him their children.

After a couple of brief spells elsewhere, William and his brother John were sent to the school which a certain Pat Frayne had started

up near their home. William later wrote a story about him, calling him Mat Kavanagh. A schoolhouse was made for him, out of turf scooped out of a bank by the road, and within a month there were a hundred scholars. Each of them brought two sods of turf for the fire every day, and this was kept burning in the middle of the school; the smoke went out through a hole in the roof. The boys took turns to sit in a circle round the fire, and there was a great deal of squabbling over this privilege.

William could make nothing of the arithmetic or the Euclid that Pat Frayne taught them, but he shone at spelling.

"These lessons always closed the business of the school, and all the boys capable of spelling were put into the class. Each boy put down a pin, which the master placed in the spelling book, and then they all took their places – forming a circle that almost went round the whole school. The head of the class was called King – the second Queen – and the third Prince. In that class I held the first place, nor do I recollect that I was ever dethroned. I went home every day with the coat sleeve of my left arm shining with the signals of my triumph."

The schoolmaster, Pat Frayne, seems to have been an engaging scoundrel. He once told his school, the day before they broke up for the Easter holiday, that he proposed to show them an astonishing sight the next day. They were each to bring him an egg, and assemble in the field by the school. He would then recite the Athanasian Creed, and lo, every egg would rise with the lightness of a soap bubble and disappear into the air.

There were a hundred children or so, and everybody came to school the next day laden with eggs. They were laid out in the field; Pat picked up one, muttered some mumbo jumbo and tossed it into the air, whereupon it crashed to the ground and broke. Pat shook his head and said the stars were against him; the miracle would have to be put off to another day. The children trooped away, too disappointed to notice at the time that the cart of the local egg merchant was standing by the field. When they came back the next day, the eggs, not surprisingly, had vanished.

Pat Frayne's school did not satisfy William. Nothing much was offered there except arithmetic (though this was well taught), and he longed for a "classical education". He told himself it was the

Latin and the Greek he wanted, but it was the stories and reading
that he was really after, and in those days classical literature was the
only literature taught in schools.

And so, in his late teens, he told his family that he was going to
Munster in the south-west of Ireland, to find his classical education.
There was great lamentation in the Carleton household as they prepared their youngest son for his quest. He lamented as much as any
of them, although the journey was of his own seeking. His mother
sewed five pound notes in the cuff of the left sleeve of his coat, and
placed thirty shillings in silver in his trouser pocket, for immediate
use. She also saw that he had a needle and thread and a penknife
so that he could rip open his sleeve and then sew it up again. On
his back he was to carry a linen knapsack, like a soldier's. The contents were for the most part books, whose shapes showed through
the linen, so that everybody could see he was a poor scholar, trudging
to find his education.

He met with much kindness on his way. Most people had great
respect for poor scholars; post-chaises stopped for him and carried
him on his journey; inns entertained him free. The only innkeeper
who charged him a farthing, he said, was a Catholic, who took a

THE POOR SCHOLAR

great interest in his soul, asked him when he had last been to confession and reminded him to say his prayers. "But notwithstanding, I had to pay thirteen pence after breakfast in the morning; that was three pence for my bed, five pence for my supper of excellent flummery and new milk the preceding night, and five more for my breakfast that morning. God knows it was cheap enough, but still, he was the only man who charged me anything."

But in spite of all this kindness his spirits dropped lower and lower the further he left home behind him. And then one morning (he had had a bad dream the night before about being pursued by a mad bull) the longing for home defeated the ambition for a classical education, and he turned to make the long journey back the way he had come. "On the morning of my return I felt as if I could tread on air, especially as I diminished the distance between me and Springton. Most fortunately, no one saw me until I entered the house – when my dear mother uttered an exclamation which it would be difficult to describe, and rushing to me with a tottering step, fainted in my arms. The tumult which ensued in the family was one of delight and joy. That day was indeed a happy day." He did not trudge the roads again for several years. When he did, he was a schoolmaster with a classical education and no one to whom to give it.

As the hedge schools were a reminder of the time when the penal laws against the Catholics had been rigorously enforced, so was the open-air Mass. During the days of the penal laws, said William Carleton, an attempt to build a Catholic chapel "would have consigned those who could dream of, much less attempt such a project, either to transportation or death." In the 1800's these penalties had lapsed, but all the same there was no chapel in all the parish where the Carletons lived. Instead there were altars covered with a little roof and open to the wind and the rain and the snow on all four sides, and beyond this knelt the congregation. In bad weather the worshippers brought trusses of hay or straw to protect their clothes from the sticky yellow clay, though there was nothing to shield them from the weather.

It was here, kneeling in a grassy ditch one Easter Sunday when he was fifteen years old, that he fell in love with Anne Duffy the miller's daughter. She was in the choir that knelt near the altar, and so was he. After Mass he followed her home adoringly. "For upwards of four years I knelt opposite her at the altar; for upwards of four

THE MIDNIGHT MASS

years my eyes were never off her, and for upwards of four years I never once, while at Mass, offered up a single prayer to heaven."

Every Sunday, when he came home, he used to go off to the glen behind the house and dream about her. The family knew it all, and would go down to rouse him when dinner time came, and William was still missing. He became a little bolder; instead of following Anne to the cross-roads after Mass, he walked all the way to her father's mill behind her. Winter and summer, for three and a half years, he followed her each week, and then turned and came home without ever having said a word. He never spoke to her, and never told her of his love; he felt it was hopeless – he could not marry her, for he had no means of supporting her.

Then one day he was sitting in front of the kitchen fire, dreaming of her, when his brother came in and asked his mother if she had heard the news, the miller's daughter had been married that morning. William felt as though he had been knocked to the ground; when he could stagger to his feet he went out to the barn and wept. It was three or four months before he recovered from the blow, and he never forgot her.

In 1847 (he was fifty-three by then) he came back to the district. He had resolved that he would not return until he had acquired fame and distinction, and it was the memory of Anne Duffy that more than anything else had spurred him on in his pursuit of it. Accompanied by a friend he walked up to the village where she had gone to live after her marriage. It was a desolate sight, for the land-owner had evicted all the inhabitants and demolished their houses in order to improve the view from his own. Anne Duffy's house was the only one that had been spared. He hesitated, and then suggested to his companion that they should call on Anne and her husband.

In all the years he had loved her he had never spoken to her of it, and he did not do so now. He turned to her husband, who was an old acquaintance, and told him that Anne "was the only woman I ever loved beyond the power of language to express," but that they had never exchanged a syllable.

" 'Well,' she replied, 'I can say on my part – and I am not ashamed to say it – that I never loved man as I loved you; but there was one thing clear, that it wasn't our fate ever to become man and wife. Had you married me it's not likely the world would have ever heard of you. As it is, I am very happily married, and lead a happy life with as good and as kind a husband as ever lived.'

"Michael laughed, and appeared rather pleased and gratified than otherwise. We then shook hands again, I took my leave, and that was my first and last interview with her whose image made the pleasure of my whole youth for nearly five years."

Elizabeth

A HIGHLAND KINGDOM

"It was in July or August then in 1803 we crossed the Spey in the big boat at Inverdruie in a perfect fever of happiness. Every mountain, every hill, every bank, fence, path, tree, cottage was known to me, every face revealed a friend . . . We were expected, so from the boat-house to the Doune it was one long gathering, all our people flocking to meet us and to shout the 'welcome home'."

Elizabeth Grant was six years old when her father brought his family back to their Highland home. They had come from London, a distance of well over 500 miles; the elder children and their parents in the family berlin with four horses ridden by two postillions in green jackets and jockey caps; the younger two and the nurses, with a footman in charge, in a heavy post-chariot behind.

"What it must have cost to have carried such a party from London to the Highlands! and how often we travelled that north road! . . . We travelled slowly, thirty miles a day on an average, starting late and stopping early, with a bait soon after noon, when we children dined."

Travelling with their own horses – Elizabeth could even remember the names of two of them, Blackbird and Smiler – they could obviously not press on as if they were going post, and changing horses throughout the journey. But even so, it was a lingering expedition; they had visited relations on the way, and had spent a few nights at Scarborough, where Elizabeth had seen the sea for the first time, and some strolling players. Sophisticated and worldly even at the age of six, she was pained by the small dirty playhouse, where they could see every streak of paint on the actors' faces and hear the prompter's voice – such a come-down after the splendours of Drury Lane and Covent Garden.

Memoirs of a Highland Lady, her memories of the first thirty-three years of her life, from childhood to her marriage, were finished when she was sixty-seven, though they had been begun twenty years or so before. By that time the tide of Victorian respectability had long since swept over England. But it had not covered Elizabeth Grant – Elizabeth Smith as she was by then. She writes in the racy, gossipy style of her youth. The gentlemen drink hard, gamble, get into debt; there are cheerful references to elopements, mistresses and illegitimate children, and mid-Victorians (the memoirs were originally written for her family) who thought that jokes referring to sea-sickness were very daring must have found some of her anecdotes startling. She tells with glee, for instance, how her uncle Ralph parodied a stage coach advertisement: "Pleasing intelligence. *The Duchess of Athole* starts every morning from the Duke's Arms at eight o'clock."

She was born two years before Mary Howitt, and died in 1885, only three years short of her. Their background was very different; the Howitts and the Bothams (Mary's parents) came from sober yeoman stock, whose parents had hardly stirred from their native parishes. The Grant blood was so blue that a silver spoon would stand up in it – as an Irish servant once remarked of his employer. They moved in high society when they were in Edinburgh and London, and at home in Rothiemurchus in the Spey valley of Inverness-shire they were the princes of a small kingdom.

Yet it was Elizabeth Grant's outlook that was the narrowest, the most wrapped up in the circles in which she moved. The Howitts flung themselves warmly into the affairs of the day: anti-slavery, politics, the literary world. Born in the 18th century, they became thoroughly Victorian. Elizabeth was a Regency figure who did not seem able to reconcile herself to the new decorum.

She flitted through the Napoleonic Wars, which had hung like a pall over Mary's childhood, much more concerned with the affairs of the innumerable Grant cousins, with the guests who filled their Highland home, and with hating her governess. She does refer to her father drilling the Highlanders on his estate: "It was a very pretty sight to come suddenly upon this fine body of men and the gay crowd collected to look at them." But the year 1815 passes without her mentioning the end of the war, and only in 1816 does she refer gloomily to "Waterloo blue", the fashionable shade of that year, "copied from the dye used in Flanders for the calico of which the peasantry made their smock-frocks or blouses. Everything new was 'Waterloo', not unreasonably . . . but to deluge us with that vile indigo, so unbecoming, even to the fairest!"

In the same way George III was remembered because of the effect

he had had on the children's clothes. His delirium had been so violent in 1812 that Elizabeth's mother had bought up a quantity of black bombazine at reduced prices. It seemed as though he would die, and people in the Grants' circle all wore mourning at royal deaths. But the king lived. "What was to be done with all the bombazine? We just had to wear it, and trimmed plentifully with crimson it did very well."

Elizabeth was a hard-headed child, not given to hero-worship. Shelley to her was the tiresome undergraduate at the Oxford college where her uncle was principal – "Mr Shelley, afterwards so celebrated, though I should think to the end half-crazy." Scott she thought little of. *Waverley* had been published in 1814: "I did not like it. The opening English scenes were to me intolerably dull and lengthy, and so prosy, and the persons introduced so uninteresting, the hero contemptible, the two heroines unnatural and disagreeable, and the whole idea given of the Highlands so utterly at variance with truth. I read it again long afterwards, and remained of the same mind." Everybody soon guessed who the anonymous author

was, she said, especially when "Mrs Scott set up a carriage, a barouche landau built in London, which from the time she got it she was seldom out of."

Elizabeth's father, John Peter Grant, owned an estate in Hertfordshire as well as the Highlands. He was a man of restless ambition, however, and looked beyond these. He had visions of himself as a great lawyer and politician, and tried his hand at both Scots and English law. The family followed him from Edinburgh to London and back again, with visits to Rothiemurchus in between whiles. It was a life that consumed a great deal of money, as did his unsatisfactory Parliamentary career.*

Elizabeth enjoyed the fashionable life in the two capitals, but she would have been perfectly content to spend all her time at the Doune – the family house on the Rothiemurchus estate. The pride of being

* He secured the rotten borough of Great Grimsby in 1812, spending enormous sums to do so. When a richer competitor ousted him in 1817, the Duke of Bedford let him sit for Tavistock until such time as one of the duke's sons was old enough for it. His political life also seriously interfered with his legal career.

a Grant and a Highlander never left her. *Memoirs of a Highland Lady* she called her book, even though only a very small part of her life was lived there, and by the time she wrote it she was settled in Ireland, managing her husband's estates.

English country people did not please her. "Uninteresting primitive families," she called the Hertfordshire squires. And the cottagers were no better – "stupid, cloddish drones, speaking a language we could not understand, and getting vacantly through their labouring lives as if existence had no pleasure." But Rothiemurchus was perfect. The people there were their own people, the farms on the estate mostly occupied by their own relations, the Doune inhabited by more of them. When Elizabeth's mother first went to the house after her marriage she found there –

"my great-uncle Sandy with his English wife, her sister, and all their carpet work, two of the five sons, an old Donald – a faithful servant of my grandfather's, who had been pensioned for his merits – an old Christy, who had gone from Strathspey to wait on my father and my aunt Lissy, and their *bonne*, good Mrs Sophy Williams. She had her pension and her attic, and so had Mr Dallas, one of the line of tutors, when he chose to come to it. Then there were college friends, bachelor cousins, and it was the fashion of the country for any of the nearer neighbours, when they came in their full dress to pay their occasional morning visits, to expect to be pressed to remain the day, often the night, as the distances are considerable in that thinly-peopled district. My father and mother never wanted for company, and the house was as full of servants as an Indian or an Irish one, strange ignorant creatures, running about in each other's way, wondering at the fine English maids who could make so little of them. Amongst the rest was a piper, who, for fear of spoiling the delicacy of the touch of his fingers, declined any work unconnected with whisky, which with plenty of oat-bread and cheese was given to all-comers all day long."

All up and down the country were humble connections who came visiting when the family were at home, and there were more relations in neighbouring counties. About twenty miles down the river was Castle Grant, where the Chief of their Clan lived. Generally about fifty people of every rank sat down to dinner at Castle Grant in the shooting season. It was entertainment in the feudal style, with the

guests at the head of the table very different to those at the bottom, who were given whisky punch to drink, not wine. Behind every chair stood a footman in gorgeous green and scarlet livery – sons of tenants, crammed into the clothes for the occasion, and quite unused to the job. The Chief presided over all, condescending to the rest of the Clan like a king.

The Grants of Rothiemurchus held court in their own territory in the same style though not on the same scale. Everyone who cared to come was made welcome. High mountains made the Spey valley remote and inaccessible, but in the birch woods and fir forests that covered it then were quantities of farms, some mere patches, others decent steadings, where relations and dependents lived. Elizabeth Grant described these farms; little cultivated spots by the burnside, with a horse or cow grazing, a cottage built of black peat with a comfortably smoking chimney, and a churn at the door. A girl might be bleaching linen in the burn, or there would be a guid-wife in a high white cap waiting to welcome any Grant who might choose to call. You could not leave such a house without drinking whisky: "at every house it must be tasted or offence would be given, so we were taught to believe . . . The very poorest cottages could offer whisky; all the men engaged in the wood manufacture drank it in goblets three times a day."

They had to be self-sufficient in this far-off kingdom.

"Our flocks and herds supplied us not only with the chief part of our food, but with fleeces to be woven into clothing, blanketing, and carpets, horn for spoons, leather to be dressed at home for various purposes, hair for the masons. Lint-seed was sown to grow into sheeting, shirting, sacking, etc. My mother even succeeded in common table linen . . . We brewed our own beer, made our own bread, made our candles; nothing was brought from afar but wine, groceries, and flour, wheat not ripening well so high above the sea. Yet we lived in luxury, game was so plentiful, red-deer, roe, hares, grouse, ptarmigan, and partridge; the river provided trout and salmon, the different lochs pike and char; the garden abounded in common fruits and common vegetables; cranberries and raspberries ran over the country, and the poultry-yard was ever well-furnished.

"Such was our Highland home; objects of interest all round us, ourselves objects of interest to all round, little princes and princesses in our Duchus, where the old feudal feelings still reigned in their deep intensity. And the face of nature so beautiful – rivers, lakes, burnies, fields, banks, braes, moors, woods, mountains, heather, the dark forest, wild animals, wild flowers, wild fruits; the picturesque inhabitants, the legends of our race, fairy tales, raids of the clans, haunted spots, cairns of the murdered – all and everything that could touch the imagination, there abounded and acted as a charm on the children of the chieftain who was adored; for my father was the father of his people, loved for himself as well as for his name."

When Elizabeth came to the Doune in 1803 in such a fever of happiness, it was to a way of life that even then was departing. It was

the last time, for instance, that she remembered all the people
assembling to shout the "welcome home". The Doune was then like
a large farmhouse, with duckpond, farm buildings and smithy all
in full view of the principal rooms, and a kitchen built of black peat
patched on to one end. This had an open chimney and bare rafters
from which one day a mouse fell into the soup. The children loved
the house like this, all so light and airy, "our nursery so enchanting
with its row of little plain deal stools – *creepies* – and our own dear
low table, round which we could ourselves place them."

But on each succeeding visit the children found "improvements";
gradually the Doune was being turned from a large Highland farmhouse into a gentleman's residence. When the children went back

69

in 1808 it was to find that the farmyard buildings had gone, the duckpond too, and the network of little streams where Elizabeth and her brother had played, and the maids had thumped their washing and laid it out to dry among the alders and hazels. The house stood on a terrace now, with fine lawns stretching round it, and in the new romantic style woodland had been cleared to make a picturesque view of the Spey.

Four more years and the Doune had changed again. Elizabeth's father had followed the fashion of the day and removed the fruit and vegetable garden some distance from the house, replacing it with a shrubbery. Elizabeth agreed that he had made everything look very beautiful, but she regretted it. She disliked having to walk a quarter of a mile on a hot summer's day just to nibble a little fruit, and thought it hard that the cook should have to send so far for a bit of thyme and parsley.

Her aunt told her that the old Highland life was dying.

"She liked the Highlands as she had known them – primitive, when nobody spoke English, when all young men wore the kilt, when printed calicoes were not to be seen, when there was no wheaten bread to be got, when she and Aunt Mary had slept in two little closets in the old house just big enough to hold them, and not big enough to hold any of their property, when there was no tidy kitchen range, no kitchen even beyond the black hut, no neat lawn, but all the work going forward about the house, the maids in the broom island with kilted coats dancing in the tubs upon the linen, and the laird worshipped as a divinity by every human being in the place."

She prophesied that old feudal affections would die out with the old customs. She was right. The same changes were coming to the Highlands as William Howitt and his contemporaries noticed in the English countryside. The gentry were becoming more sophisticated, they were drawing away from the country folk. Both had been united by a common interest in the land on which they lived; now they were dividing.

Elizabeth started to keep a journal to try to show her aunt that life could still be happier among their Inverness mountains than elsewhere, and that indeed much went on as before.

There was the kirk, filled to overflowing with "our own people" –

men who had known her grandfather and great-grandfather; younger men, lads, and boys, all in the tartan. "The plaid as a wrap, the plaid as a drapery, with kilt to match on some, blue trews on others, blue jackets on all." The women were plaided too, the older women in high white caps, the younger ones bare-headed, with neatly braided hair, and few of them in shoes or stockings.

There was a service only every three weeks, and as the minister had only two sermons, they came to know them well. The Grant family went to the English service – the Gaelic one came first. It was not conducted with much ceremony. The minister would drone out a few lines of the psalms, and then hand his book to the precentor, who got up and announced the tune. The practice was that he screeched the first line, which was repeated by the congregation, and so, turn and turn about to the end of the psalm, everybody following his own whim so far as singing went. "The dogs seized this occasion to bark (for they always came to the kirk with the family), and the babies to cry. When the minister could bear the din no longer he popped up again, again leaned over, touched the precentor's head, and instantly all sound ceased."

Then the minister would pray. He was a violent Tory, and intensely disliked having to pray for the Hanoverian family, so he cut that business as short as possible: – "God bless the King, and all the Royal Family; as Thou hast made them great make them GOOD." During the sermon that followed, the men took snuff. "They fed their noses with quills fastened by strings to the lids of their mulls, spooning up the snuff in quantities and without waste. The old women snuffed too, and groaned a great deal, to express their mental sufferings, their grief for all the backslidings supposed to be thundered at from the pulpit; lapses from faith was their grand self-accusation, lapses from virtue were, alas! little commented on; temperance and chastity were not in the Highland code of morality."

Another minister in the locality, known to everybody as Parson John, was a merry little man, a great hand at eating, even better at good drinking, but not so skilled at sermons. When he ran out of improving things to say, he would turn to the news. It was wartime, and there were plenty of stirring events to report – though by the time news reached Inverness-shire it might have become rather garbled.

"The parson gave it as he got it, and one Sunday delivered a marvellous narrative of passing events. Finding out during the week his error, he hastened honestly to correct it, so, on the following Sunday, after the psalm and the prayer and the solemn giving out of the text, he raised his hands and thus addressed his flock, 'My brethren, it was a' lees I told ye last Sabbath day.' ' "

All this was the 18th century style, and as the new century wore on the services became far more decorous. The kirks, which Elizabeth remembered as being in a ruinous state with falling roofs and weed-choked graveyards, were rebuilt; the ministers became far graver, and the Highlander who in those early days believed as much in fairy legends, old clan tales and superstitions as in the Bible, became more concerned with kirk matters – those who still attended, that is, for by the middle of the century Elizabeth was lamenting how small the congregation was in the now neat kirk.

In the old style, too, were the harvest homes. There were four large farms on the Rothiemurchus land, and the Grants celebrated the harvest at three of them. Their favourite took place at the Dell.

"My father and mother and all of us, stuffed into or on the carriage, drove there to dinner, which was served in the best parlour, my father at the head of the table, Duncan Macintosh [the farmer] at the foot, and those for whom there was not room at the principal board went with at least equal glee to a side table. There was always broth, mutton boiled and roasted, fowls, muirfowl* – three or four pair on a dish – apple-pie and rice pudding, such jugs upon jugs of cream, cheese, oatcakes and butter; thick bannocks of flour instead of wheaten bread, a bottle of port, a bottle of sherry, and after dinner no end of whisky punch.

"In the kitchen was all the remains of the sheep, broth, haggis, head and feet singed, puddings black and white, a pile of oaten cakes, a kit of butter, two whole cheeses, one tub of sowans,* another of curd, whey and whisky in plenty. The kitchen party, including any servants from house or farm that could be spared so early from [neighbouring households] dined when we had done, and we ladies, leaving the gentlemen to their punch, took a view of the kitchen festivities before retiring to the bedroom of Mrs Macintosh to make the tea."

* Red grouse.   * Boiled fermented oats.

"When the gentlemen joined us the parlour was prepared for dancing. With what ecstasies we heard the first sweep of that masterly bow across my father's Cremona! The first strathspey was danced by my father and Mrs Macintosh; if my mother danced at all, it was later in the evening. My father's dancing was peculiar – a very quiet body, and very busy feet, they shuffled away in double quick time steps of his own composition . . . My mother did better, she moved quietly in Highland matron fashion, for however lightly the lasses footed it, etiquette forbade the wives to do more than 'tread the measure'. William and Mary moved in the grave style of my mother; Johnnie without instruction danced beautifully; Jane was perfection, so light, so active, and so graceful . . ."

There were many occasions like these – funeral feasts, house-warmings, country dances (there was an especially good one that followed a cattle market) – when people of every rank met on terms of great friendliness, and some of the fine manners of the more sophisticated rubbed off on the country folk. This was the old Highland tradition, but it was departing, as Elizabeth's aunt had prophesied. By mid-Victorian times it was a thing of the past. "The few grandees shut themselves up rigorously in their proud exclusiveness . . . Each section appears now to keep apart, unnoticed by the class above, and in turn not noticing the class below."

Unconsciously Elizabeth's father was playing a part in the breaking of the old tradition. The Doune had been turned from a farm-

house into a fine mansion. It had been bare and light and empty
before; now it was curtained and carpeted and opulently furnished.
It had acquired a magnificent library, with busts and vases above
the bookshelves, and folios full of valuable prints. The first floor
drawing room, where the grand piano and the harp stood, looked
down on to beautiful views of the Spey. Town manners had invaded
the country. Mr Grant tried too to civilize the people on the estate.
Some of them liked the pretty little model cottages he built; four
old wives did not. "Old, smoke-dried, shrivelled-up witches with
pipes in their mouths, and blankets on their backs, they preferred
the ingle-nook in their dark, dirty, smoke-filled huts to this picture
of comfort." It was not long before they had "accidentally" set it
on fire.

It took a great deal of money, of course. There were not only the
improvements at Rothiemurchus, but gay society life in Edinburgh
to pay for, when Mrs Grant filled every evening with dinner parties
and balls, and the girls were the envy of all their contemporaries
with their London-made clothes. But nobody worried; timber from

style, trying to pay off the debts with sales of more and more timber

The first inkling that Elizabeth had of the disastrous state of her father's affairs was when she was twenty-three. They were in a rented house in Edinburgh. One morning the younger daughters were dispatched on a visit, the servants were all sent on errands, and Mrs Grant then broke it to Elizabeth that the bailiffs were coming to seize what property they could. They found little when they came, as the furniture was hired, but they marked down the piano and her father's law library.

The family was distressed and shaken, but they still thought that their difficulties were temporary, and the Rothiemurchus forests inexhaustible. The father rented another Edinburgh house; the rest of the family went back to Rothiemurchus, and here William, the eldest son, tried his best to put the affairs of the estate into order, and the girls to see that the house was run in a less wasteful way. The children all loved the Highland life and they amused themselves much as before. "We would rush out of doors, be off to fish, or to visit our thousand friends, or to the forest or to the mill, or to take a row upon the loch, unmooring the boat ourselves, and Jane and I handling the oars just as well as our brothers . . . We were so happy, so busy, we felt it an interruption when there came visitors."

The real truth dawned on Elizabeth one day when she was out on a forest excursion.

"My rough pony was led through the moss of Achnahatanich by honest old John Bain. We were looking over a wide, bare plain, which the last time I had seen it had been all wood; I believe I started; the good old man shook his grey head, and then, with more respect than usual in his manner, he told all that was said, all that he feared, all that some one of us should know, and that he saw 'it was fixed that Miss Lizzie should hear, for though she was lightsome she would come to sense when it was wanted to keep her mamma easy, try to help her brothers, and not refuse a good match for herself.'"

Poor Elizabeth now regretted her lost opportunities and her thoughtless extravagances. But as far as making a good match was concerned, she felt that the time for that was long past; she was twenty-five after all.

Somehow the family lived on at Rothiemurchus in much the usual

the Rothiemurchus forests would pay for all that was needed.
from the fast diminishing forests. But by 1826 these amounted to
£60,000, and the eldest son, William, was in prison for debts he had
himself incurred at college. Then the grey hand of poverty did begin
to pinch the Doune. Most of the servants had gone; the two that
were left waited patiently to be paid. There were few stores left in
the house, and the Inverness tradesmen now refused to supply their
orders.

Elizabeth and her sister Mary tried to earn a few pounds by
writing. They crouched in an attic in the driest part of the house,
for the rain and the snow were now pouring through the neglected
roof. Here by the light of candle stumps and sticks they had themselves gathered from the plantations they sat and scribbled through
the long northern hours of darkness. They were lucky, or perhaps
they had influential friends, and the articles they wrote were sold.
They spent the few pounds they made on new shoes, and on paying
the maids, and even put a little by.

But the end had come. The Duke of Bedford now wanted the
Tavistock constituency for his own son.* John Peter Grant's parliamentary career was at an end and his creditors closed in on him like
vultures.

"He left us; he never returned to his Duchus. When he drove away
to catch the coach that lovely summer morning, he looked for the
last time on those beautiful scenes he dearly loved and most certainly

* Lord John Russell, uncle of Frederic Hamilton, see page 204.

76

was proud of, though he never valued his inheritance rightly. He went first to London and then abroad."

But his friends did what they could for him, and one of them, by reminding George IV that he had drunk the unique Grant whisky on his visit to Edinburgh in 1822, secured for him an Indian judgeship. So the Doune was to be emptied of all Grants and let to strangers. Everything except the furniture, and the clothes they needed, was to be auctioned. It was difficult even to find money to take them to India, but a kind neighbour helped, and there was a little money from the girls' writings. On the last day Elizabeth and Mary walked out to see their last of Rothiemurchus – the pretty gardens, all banks and braes and little dells with birch woods, then the wood and the burn beyond; further still the loch where they had so often rowed, and their own play cottage on its bank. They did not cry until they were nearly home, and a certain green gate had closed behind them. "I shall hear it till I die; it seemed to end the poetry of our existence." At five o'clock on that August day of 1827 the Grants left Rothiemurchus.

"No one till that moment knew that we were to go that evening, there was therefore no crowd; the few servants from the farm, joined by the two maids from the house, watched us crossing in the little boat, to which Mary and I walked down alone behind the others. Crossing the hall, William had caught up an old plaid of my father's to put upon the seat of the boat; he called old John Macintosh to row us over. When leaving the boat, my mother threw the plaid over the bewildered old man's shoulders. He knew it was the Laird's, and I heard he was buried in it. We entered the carriage, never once looked back, nor shed a tear; very gravely we made out those eight miles among the hills and woods, and heaths and lochs, and the dear Spey, all of which we had loved from childhood and which never again could be the same to any of us."

Elizabeth, Mary and their mother joined their father in India. There both the girls met their future husbands. Elizabeth returned in 1830, Miss Grant of Rothiemurchus no longer, but Mrs Smith of Baltiboys. Henceforward she was to give all her energy and sympathies to caring for the people on her husband's Irish estate. Rothiemurchus was behind her, and when she visited it many years later it seemed strange and remote.

William Howitt

A ROMANTIC WANDERER

"OUR day pursuits were as full of interest to me as our evening ones. I remember getting up of a winter moonlight morning at about four o'clock, and going off to examine my mole traps set in distant fields, take out the moles caught, and reset the traps. Such zest has the young mind in what it engages in. My days used to be joyfully spent in driving the plough, helping to hack up frozen turnips for the sheep and cattle, helping to cut hay and fill racks and cribs with hay and straw for horses and cows. Early in spring, about March, I used to be up betimes in the still, bitter frosty mornings to look after the ewes and their lambs.

"As the spring advanced, my employments were weeding corn, driving the plough, and helping to hoe crops. I used to delight in listening to the stories of the labourers, who were long employed on the farm, and seemed almost to make part of the family; and remembering those times, I can well understand what a vast amount of pleasure is enjoyed amid youth and health in country life. . . .

"Then came, in their season, mowing, mushroom-gathering in the pastures, nutting in the woods, collecting acorns for the swine in

their bucketsful as they pattered down on a windy day from the trees; threshing, taking in corn-stacks, and killing rats and mice, collecting hen, duck, geese, and guinea-fowl eggs. Then came jolly Christmas, with its gathering together of old and young; blind-man's buff, hunt-the-slipper, forfeits, mince-pie eating, and fishing for the ring in the great posset-pot."

Mary Howitt's childhood was sober and sedate; William's is a record of boisterous high spirits. He left an account of himself in a chapter of his wife's autobiography, and of his boyhood in *The Boy's Country Book* (1839). The French wars that overshadowed Mary's childhood seemed to make no mark on William; his talk is of the joy of the English country life. His feeling for it never left him; years later, when he was an old man living in Italy, he could not admire the glories of Rome for thinking wistfully of English hawthorn hedges.

He was born in 1792. There were seven Howitt boys in the family, living in the comfortable large Derbyshire farmhouse. Their fore-bears had been a turbulent lot, but with their father, Thomas Howitt who became a Quaker, the family had taken a turn for the better. The Howitts however were Quakers of quite a different sort from the Bothams; their religion cast no gloom on them, nor did they see any reason why they should not mix freely with the outside world.

Impetuous, warm-hearted and hot-headed, William in adult life went chasing off after many different interests. But he had a family to support, and so he wrote diligently, year in and year out, until from a joyful enthusiasm it became a burden. His early books about the country – landscapes, seasons, people, and way of life – are much his best, and of these perhaps his own memories of the midlands in his youth stand out. We get a picture of an untamed English country-side where you could wander for a day seeing nobody, where town manners and town ways were unknown. Farmers were not gentlemen in those days, they were sturdy, hard-working yeomen who worked beside their farmhands and sat down to eat with them in their kitchens; and the cottagers were a tougher, more independent lot than they later became when they had to rely on the local squire for their living.

On his grey pony, Peter Scroggins, William was allowed to range at will. "I felt myself a famous man," he wrote, "with a pony of my own and liberty to ride him when and where I could." He led the village boys in the wildest japes. There were the usual bird-nesting and tree-climbing adventures. There were also more serious ones, such as the occasion when he and some companions started plunder-ing a pheasant preserve and got caught in one of the man-traps that were still legal then. They spent a dreadful night in the keeper's cottage, and were dragged next morning before the landowner (who,

in the style of the times, was also the local magistrate). "O the dismal sinking and knocking of our hearts! We were to appear before the magistrate as poachers and vagabonds – to be punished – perhaps transported! – our fears suggested – perhaps to be hanged!" However, the magistrate recognized them, tattered and coated with mud and dust, as the sons of acquaintances and they were dismissed. If they had been mere village boys they might well have been transported.

Of those memories of the expeditions of his youth, two stand out: the time when he saw Byron's house, and the time when he and his pony wandered into the mining area.

He was only four years younger than Byron, but his imagination was drunk with him. He had avidly read, not only the poems which had been published in 1807, but also the satirical retort to the critics who had denounced them, "which appeared to me the grandest piece of poetical justice ever inflicted on the critics." At the Howitts' home of Heanor, only nine miles off, they knew all about the wild doings of the young lord and his companions at Newstead Abbey. They also knew – the whole countryside knew – the reputation of the old lord, his great-uncle, who was supposed to have erected a statue to the devil in the garden, and had cut down the trees so as to damage the estate as much as he could before Byron's father could inherit it. Thomas Howitt had indeed picked two young poplar-trees out of a cart-load torn up on the Newstead property by the old lord in his devastating fury, as the cart passed through Heanor, and had planted them in a field by his own house.

When William first saw Newstead, he was living, not at home, but in Mansfield on the edge of Sherwood Forest. He was seventeen years old, and his father, who was full of high-minded theories about what his boys should do (inspired by readings of Rousseau), had decided that he ought to learn a craft before he entered a profession. Carpentry it should be, and then William could become an architect. William had no inclination to be either, but he was perfectly happy to be apprenticed to a carpenter in Mansfield, because it gave him opportunities to explore part of the country that was new to him.

"I had frequently to carry out bills to country-houses, an errand that I very much liked, for it gratified my fondness for rambling through the country and the villages, and amongst the old English halls, then inhabited, long before the days of railroads, by rude squires that rarely reached London, but spent their lives in hunting and shooting. I was sent one summer's day to Kirkby and Linby. These were primitive farming villages buried in trees, and as old-world and obscure as possible.

"Returning from these sleepy hollows of old Nottinghamshire agricultural villages, where the quiet, the thick foliage, and the slumber of ages seemed to brood', my way lay past Newstead. It would be difficult to describe my sensations as the view of the abbey opened upon me. First, I came upon the lake below, lying in the wide valley, where the old lord, as he was called, the poet's grand-uncle, had piled up artificial rocks, and in which had been found the brazen eagle thrown into it by the monks as they fled at the locking-up of their establishment in Henry VIII's time. There stood forth the western front of the old abbey, with its large window of Early English style, and the queer old fountain, with its quaint figures of animals on the green in front; and to the left another lake, an old water-mill, and sham fortifications. All was silent, no soul anywhere was visible. . . ."

[Boldly Howitt rang a bell on a door in the front] "All continued silent; I then seized a queer old knocker and gave a lusty pounding. Within, the sound was re-echoed with a strange hollow dreariness, indicating emptiness and solitude. At length a little wicket opened in the door, and an ancient visage presented itself, took a survey of me, and asked my business. I replied I was a great admirer of the poet, and, casually passing, would much like to see the house and garden. This was old Murray, the sole occupant of the abbey in the lord's absence. He asked how many persons there were; and on my replying only myself, he gave a sort of unsatisfactory 'Humph!' and I thought my chance was gone. But the sight of a half-crown, which I showed at the wicket, turned the scale. He opened the door, saying he was just cooking his dinner, but I might go into the garden, and when he had finished his dinner he would come to me. Nothing could have suited me better. I told him not to hurry; I could amuse myself in examining the gardens as long as he pleased. He opened a side-door, and descending some steps, I was alone in a perfect wilderness.

"I was just behind the western façade of the abbey church. The church was gone, but the front was left, like a tall screen, with its great window, its pinnacles, buttresses, and carvings. Before me, in what once was the nave, but now a plot of bushes and tall grass, stood conspicuously the dog's tomb. . . . Before me lay the old gardens, which I entered: there was a large pond, long, straight walks all overgrown with weeds, and the shrubs and bushes of both flower and kitchen gardens, roses, lilies, gooseberries, and currant-bushes all smothered by a wild growth of Nature's sowing. The place appeared left entirely to itself. There was no trace of human hand or foot anywhere. Towards the end of the gardens I passed under alleys moss-grown and over-shadowed, made, in fact, dim and gloomy with trees, and there I discovered what the simple country people had called 'the old lord's devils.' They were merely leaden statues of fauns, satyrs, and other rural creatures of mythology.

"I had scarcely made my round when old Murray appeared, and

took me through the house. What struck me sensibly was the ruin that was fast hurrying through the building again. Byron had replenished the house in a somewhat showy style, without first repairing the roof, and the rains had poured in over gilded cornices, great mirrors, and rich silken curtains. In the kitchen were painted upon the wall over the ample fireplace words that, according to Byron's own account and that of others, had been very little regarded: 'Waste not, want not.' In the drawing room stood in a cabinet the celebrated skull cup, and over the fireplace the full-length portrait of Byron in a sailor's dress. . . . In his study, though the books were gone, there remained two tall graceful stands of wood, on which were placed very perfect and finely polished skulls, and betwixt these hung on the wall a crucifix, as though he had been a Catholic."

[About a year later, riding over Sherwood Forest,] "I saw a young gentleman approaching leading his horse. Looking attentively at him, I observed that he limped on one foot, and it instantly occurred to me – Lord Byron! . . . I could recognize him not only by his limp, but by the portrait I had seen at the abbey."

It was the only time he was ever to see him. About fifteen years later, his admiration for the poet still undimmed, he and Mary stood by his coffin. Byron's body had been brought back from Greece, and it lay at Nottingham for a night before it was taken for burial to the family vaults. William joined the procession that went from Nottingham to Hucknall, tramping through the hot midday sun, and raging at the lack of respect and decency that was shown at the funeral ceremonies.

"Rest in thy tomb, young heir of glory, rest," he wrote, pouring out his emotions, and his indignation that so few seemed to share them.

"And thy great memory with deep feeling fill
Those scenes which thou hast trod, and hallow every hill."

Deeply moved he might have been, but he was not a great poet. He was far better at describing the things that he had seen. One of his most remarkable pieces of writing is his account of an industrial landscape at the turn of the century. Very strange and primitive it seems to us now, and it was altogether marvellous to a country boy, though the Derbyshire coalfields were in fact not very far from his home.

"I first saw the coal-pits by night. As I rode over a hill I suddenly perceived before me, in every direction, strange lights, that only seemed to make the darkness deeper. Melancholy sounds, as of groans and sighings, and wild lamentings, came upon my ear, and fell awfully upon my heart. I could perceive by the fires, that blazed here and there in a hundred places, that a wild landscape was before me, and Durman, the young man I have mentioned, told me it was full of coal-pits; that these fires were burning by them; and that the sounds I heard were the sounds of the machinery by which the coal was drawn up, and of the steam-engines by which the pits were cleared of water. As we went on we soon approached one of the coal-pits, and a wild scene it was. In two or three tall cressets fires were flaming and flickering in the wind; on the ground other large fires were burning, and by their light I could see black figures standing or moving about. Around were other paler fires, that with a smothered force seemed burning dimly, and every now and then breaking up with a stream of flame, and then dying away again. The flames gleamed ruddily on the colliers: on their great wailing wheels and tall timbers; and on the immense stacks of coals that stood around.

"It required daylight and further acquaintance with the place and people to dispel my awe. When these came, and I had looked about me, I discovered many objects of interest. I found that the smothered fires that I had seen were coke fires; that is, fires in which

85

they burn the soft coal to coke or mineral charcoal, in the same way that in the forests they burn wood into charcoal. . . . I found the pits awful circular gulphs of some yards wide, and of an immense depth; some sixty or seventy yards, others as much as two hundred yards. A terrible place one of these pits seemed to me, far more than those old forsaken ones where I had gone to seek birds'-nests, because those were half concealed with bushes; and these standing wide open to the day. I shuddered to see the colliers go near them, much more to see them seat themselves on a single chain, hook it to the end of the huge rope that hung over this terrible chasm, and suffer themselves to be thus let down to the bottom.

"These pits were very old-fashioned pits. They were not worked by steam-engines, which in those days merely drew water, but by which the coals are now whirled up, and the men are whirled down with a fearful speed. They were worked only by a huge wheel, with one end of its axle on the earth, and the other fixed to the beam above. This wheel, which they call a gin, was turned round by a couple of horses; and a large rope uncoiling one way as it coiled the other round the gin, drew up the coal, and let down the chain for more at the same time. At the mouth of the pit a man stood with an iron hook, and as the coal came up piled on a sledge called a cauf, and secured by wooden frames called garlands, he seized the ring in the end of the cauf and drew the coal to land. At one of these pits a girl once performed this office, and missing her foot as she approached the pit mouth to hook the load of coal, plunged headlong into the pit and was dashed to pieces. But what was the most sad of all was, that the person who was the first at the bottom to hear her fall, and who came and found the mangled corpse, was her own father.

"On every pit-hill, as they call it, that is, on the mound that surmounts the pit, made by the earth thrown out in digging it, the colliers have a cabin, often built of coal. In this they keep a good fire in cold weather, and here when they have done their work they often sit and drink ale and make merry. A rude and uncouth crew they look; yet I found them a very honest, good-natured set of fellows; and I delighted to sit on a great coal with them, and hear them tell their country stories. . . .

"Many a day did I use to spend amongst these black and honest mortals. I used to climb upon their stacks of coals, that extended far and wide, a sable wilderness, and there I found many a treasure of wagtails' nests. At length I mustered courage to go down a pit – yes, down one of those dreadful gulphs of which no bottom could be seen, but up which came a thin blue vapour, and a sound of falling waters. I was arrayed in a flannel frock, such as the colliers all wear, lent me by a pit-boy, and a round crowned hat without brim, well stuffed with hay. In this guise a collier seated himself on the chain, and taking me on his knee, we were swung off over the pit-mouth. Oh! it was a terrible moment, and made me sick and giddy. The rope appeared to dwindle to a hair, and below I dared not look, but I thought to what a horrible unknown depth I was going! Down, however, we went. Around us gushed water from the bricks which lined the side of the pit, and fell with a dreary, splashing sound, far, far below. Anon, I looked up – the daylight appeared only a small circular, intense speck, like a star above me; and presently I heard below human voices sounding deeply like echoes. To my vast delight we soon felt the solid ground beneath us. A collier unhooked my protector from his chain, and we stood at the entrance of a region of darkness.

"What a wild, gloomy, and strange scene! A black cavern of immense extent was before me, shewn by a few glimmering lights. We went on a good way; when, suddenly, I saw two rows of lights burning, one on the right, the other on the left. These were the lights by which the colliers were at work getting the coal. The face of the coal where they work they call a benk. One is the deep benk, the other is the basset benk. Here the poor fellows sit on the ground, with their sharp picks, undermining a certain quantity of the coal measured and marked out with chalk, or in their language, – holing a stint. Then comes the hammer-man with his hammer, and driving his wedge in above, down comes the mass of coal, and they load it on the cauf and garlands, and a little pony draws it along a little railway to the pit-mouth where it is drawn up for use. As the poor fellows clear away the coal, they prop the roof up with pieces of wood, called puncheons, or the earth above them would fall in and bury them; and this it sometimes does in spite of all their care, and they are crushed to death, or are left alive beneath the immense mass to perish of famine before their friends can dig them out."

William was horrified by the dangers, yet excited. His imagination was seized by the immensity of the new worlds that coal and steam were opening. It was beautiful, wonderful, magical, to see Tyneside coal wagons at Newcastle running along rails from the pits to empty themselves into the holds of ships below. A pit-head at night, dense with smoke, the steam engines clanking and crashing and the huge boilers hissing was "a scene as wild and fearful as painter or poet could wish to see." But these were early days; you could still hear the cuckoo and the corncrake on the plain where the long coal trains were dragged whistling and screaming. He wrote of these wonders in *The Rural Life of England* in 1838. He was to live to see that rural life gradually overwhelmed and disappearing; the new magic had taken possession of its masters.

End of the straitt or platform, along which the baskets, filled with coal, are brought on a rail-road from the mines, with the spout through which they are discharged into the vessel.

Alexander

THE RAGGED RADICAL WHO
RAN AWAY

"SHOULD you ever be in Scotland and see Springfield, you will find a row of shabby looking tiled sheds, such they continued to be when I was last there, the centre one of which is about twelve feet by fourteen, and not so high in the walls as will allow a man to get in without stooping. That place without ceiling, or anything beneath the bare tiles of the roof; without a floor save the common clay; without a cupboard or recess of any kind; with no grate but the iron bars which the tenants carried to it, built up and took away when they left it; with no partition of any kind save what the beds made; with no window save four small panes on one side – it was this house, still a hind's house at Springfield, for which, to obtain leave to live in, my mother sheared the harvest and carried the stacks.

"How eight children and father and mother were huddled in that place is not easily told. The worst of it was, that food was so very dear, clothes were so very dear, as to us not to be obtainable, and national glory was so very dear – that glory which Europe was mad about at that time, and for which we, like others, had to pay, that even those bare walls, for which so much of my mother's labour had to be paid in rent, were less comfortable than they might have been."

This was the hut in which Alexander Somerville was born in Berwickshire, in the Scottish Lowlands, in 1811. Everybody knew him as Sandy. He was the eleventh child, and came, as he wrote in *The Autobiography of a Working Man* in 1848, at a time when he could very well have been spared. His father was a farm labourer who never earned more than 15s. (75p.) in a week (and usually less); so was his mother, and as their hut depended on her work, she carried the sheaves from the stackyard into the barn all the winter before Alexander was born, and the winter after. A little brother brought the baby to her to be suckled.

It was a struggle even to keep alive; Alexander could remember how when once hungry cattle from the stackyard broke into the house and ate the family's store of potatoes even his stout-hearted mother sat down and wept, for there was now no food left, nor any prospect of more.

But Alexander's father did not allow himself to be dragged down by the circumstances in which he lived. There is a fighting quality, an inner toughness in the northerner which keeps his head high in conditions which would defeat a weaker spirit. It is noticeable throughout the 19th century how much better the northern farm labourer did than the labourer in the south. Some have said it was because the farm worker in the south had his morale destroyed by dependence on a landowner; others have thought it was due to better education, and the way the Presbyterian church was organized, so that the poorest could be an elder.

Certainly Alexander's father believed in education. He might not be able to buy clothes for his children, and he could not afford the shilling to pay the parish clerk to have the name of his eleventh child put on the parish registers, but he scraped together the pence to send them to school. And in that miserable shed, twelve by fourteen feet, occupied by eight children and two adults, he never neglected to have family worship at night – a prayer, a psalm, a Bible reading, and a long extempore prayer – and family prayers and his "private duty" in the morning.

"The wettest, windiest, and coldest storm that ever blew in those regions did not keep him from the meeting-house on the Sabbath, no

matter what the distance might be, and the distance from most places where he lived was from five to ten miles; though deeply imbued with religious sentiments at all times, and though struggling with poverty on one side, and his affectionate love for his family on the other, continually, yet was he one of the most lively companions to work with, or walk with, always ready with an anecdote that had a point in it. At the annual 'winter suppers', or the 'kirnes' – harvest homes – which our master gave to his workpeople, my father was always the life of the company; ready with droll stories, witty jokes, and songs with a meaning in them; the only drawback on his pleasure was that these festivities being usually held on Saturday night (that the master might not lose the work of any of his men through intemperate headaches the next day), he felt the more serious responsibility of encroaching on the Lord's Day. No persuasion nor entreaty, nor enjoyment of fun, nor the trick of putting the clock back, would keep him after ten o'clock. Nor would he allow any of us to remain later. We were always on those occasions taken home to have family worship over, and be in bed by twelve."

These were a very different sort of Scots from Elizabeth Grant's Highlanders, whose religion was mostly one of legends, and superstitions and fairy tales. Religious controversy was meat and drink to Alexander's father, and somehow he had acquired a small library of theological books, mostly controversy, with a few volumes of sermons. He had friends who were just as devoted to learning. There was Robert Wallace, whose wife had taught him to read after marriage. He had never seen the stars through a telescope, but he knew all that books could tell him of the celestial system. What Robert Wallace loved to do on a Sunday was to take a wheaten flour loaf scooped out and filled with treacle or sugar, and find some secluded place in a field where he could lie and read about astronomy and eat his bread and treacle. Then there was an old blind man called James Dawson who had read history and geography extensively when he had had the eyes to see books. He would talk to historical characters as though they were there, arguing with Raleigh and Essex and Burleigh; and young Alexander, herding the cattle for his parents, would listen to him and learn.

Probably he learned more from James Dawson than ever he did from school, and certainly it was more pleasant learning. He had been taught to read at home, and did not go to school until he was eight, partly because it was two miles away, and partly because until that year, 1818, when prices fell a little, it was not possible to find clothes fit to send him in.

Even so, he presented a strange little figure at Birnyknows school. He was not wearing the usual corduroy suit, but some clothes remade

from some cast-offs given to an elder brother a year or two before.
"There was a brown coat which had been reduced in size, but it
was still too large for me; trousers which had once been of a very
light blue or grey, and an infirm hat." The infirm hat was his greatest
grief. It had a very broad brim; his mother had tried to cut some of
this so that he could at least see below it, but it still looked extraordinary, and the other boys hooted and jeered. It was the sight of
him in his cut-down, patched clothes and his huge, flapping hat
that made the other boys cast him as "the ragged radical" in the
new game that they devised.

"Perhaps, before I go further," wrote Alexander Somerville in the
autobiography that he originally intended to be for his young son,
"I should tell you who and what the radicals were. They were people
who complained that the country was not governed as it should be,
that the laws were not made by those who should have made the
laws. They were grieved to be excluded from voting for members of
parliament, and they felt at the same time that food was dear, wages
low, and taxation very high. They said that those circumstances
must be altered, and in changing them they must go to the root of
the evil and effect a radical change . . . The great body of the radicals
was composed of honest working people; but there were attached

to them a few persons of wealth and high social station, while all below the working classes, that is to say, the idle, and dissolute, and the rambling makers of speeches, who went from town to town exciting the industrious people to rise against the law and effect a radical reformation, or revolution, by force of guns, pistols, and pikes, were as a matter of course called, and were proud to be called radicals. . . .''

There was much talk in Birnyknows school in the winter of 1819 of what the boys would all do if the terrible set of men called radicals came. The sons of farmers who took newspapers told dark stories of their frightful deeds, how they were threatening to take the lives and destroy the property of all good people. "And then one boy would say he was not afraid of the radicals, for he had an uncle who was a soldier, and another had a brother a soldier, and a farmer's son would say that his father was in the yeomanry and had a sword, and saddle with holster pipes, and pistols in the holster pipes, and neither he nor his father were afraid, he would get his father to kill all the radicals who offered to touch him, for they were only ragged weavers, half starved and not able to fight; and the other boys whose brothers and uncles were soldiers, would say that they would go to such a brother or such uncle, and get him to kill the radicals that offered to touch them.''

And so the "ragged radical" game was invented. The boys were to divide themselves into two parties, radicals and soldiers. The sons of the farmers made themselves the soldiers, and picked the radicals from the boys who had the shabbiest clothes. This meant Alexander, and on that first day he went home with the brim torn from his hat, his trousers split up, and all the buttons torn from his waistcoat.

"When I went home on that first evening of my ragged radicalship, my poor mother stood aghast, lifted her hands, and said, in a tone of despair, 'What shall I do with those rags?' They were stripped off, I got an early supper and was sent to bed, while she began to mend them – putting in a piece there and a piece here, sewing up a rent, darning the worn holes, and ending some hours after midnight, not far from the usual hour of rising from bed, by sewing the luckless brim upon my infirm hat. Her motherly affection for me, and natural pride in the good appearance of her family, had led her to suggest to my father that I should not be sent again to school until we had got the 'siller' we were waiting for to get new clothes. But my father, though not less affectionate, and not less anxious about the appearance of his family, was stern upon that point. 'If the laddie lives to be a man,' said he, 'he will need his education, and more than we can give him. If I had got schooling myself, as I am trying to give to all my sons, it would have helped me through the world more easily than I have got through. The laddie must go to the school."

And so Alexander set off for school next morning, his mother begging him with tears not to get his clothes torn again. But "soldiers and radicals" was again the game, and as soon as he appeared the soldiers charged him, and knocked the hat over his eyes with his head through its crown. Then they seized him to carry him off to be hanged and beheaded. "I made a violent effort to free myself, and the rents of yesterday, which my mother had so carefully sewed, broke open afresh. The hat I raised from where it had sunk over my face, and saw part of the brim in the hands of a lad who was a kind of king of the school, or cock of the walk, with some of my poor mother's threads hanging from it."

Alexander had never fought or had heard of fighting till he went to school. But now his blood was hot. He knocked down the king of the school and laid about some of the others. Someone ran for

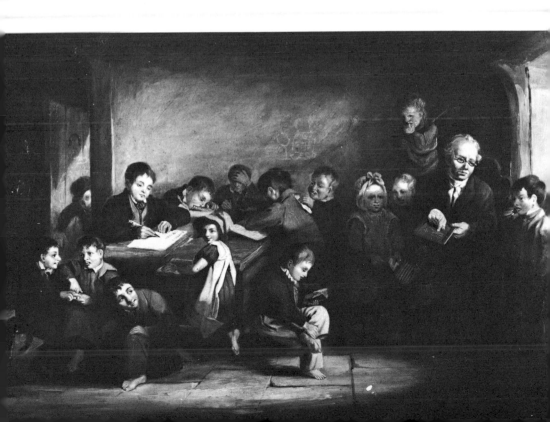

the schoolmaster, and when Alexander went in, with face bloodied and clothes torn, there he was with his terrible taws. Six cuts were given, on each hand ("He had a way of raising himself upon his toes when he swung the heavy taws round his head, and came down upon his feet with a spring, giving the cuts slantingly on the hand") Alexander made it worse for himself by stubbornly refusing to cry out, and he was beaten about the head and body until he was driven on to the heap of coals in the corner of the school, where he had to stay until the evening.

"The day was piercing cold. The house was an old place, with no furniture nor partition in it. I sat at the end farthest from the fire-place, and near to the door, which was an old door that did not fit its place, and which allowed the wind to blow freely through. It blew through and about me as if it had been another school-master, and was as partial to the farmers' sons, and as cruel to the ragged boys of farm labourers, as he was."

But the worst misery to Alexander came at the end of the day. It was Friday when the weekly marks were read, and the boys who had no bad marks chalked up against them were rewarded with a half-penny, and those who went through the spelling test without a mistake went up to the top of the class.

"I spelt all my own share of the words; and the words which others stuck at, on their being put to me, I spelt for them. I was in hopes that this good work on my part would lead to my free pardon, and redemption from the coal-hole, and I watched with tremulous expectation the reading of the names of my class. The teacher called silence, and when silence was obtained, he began slowly and emphatically, 'the bad boy who sits on the coals, *none*; at the *bottom* of the class, and to sit on the coals until he behaves better.' And the next, who had several marks to his name, was read off thus – 'at the top of the class in the bad boy's place.' I can hardly say if I would not have had another thrashing with the taws rather than have suffered this renewed disgrace."

One good resulted from this sad story – the infirm hat was now beyond repair, and "some old highland bonnet, which once belonged to James or Peter, was rummaged out and mended for me. This,

though it did not come over my ears as the ample hat had done, saved me from that biting ridicule which was worse than biting frost." For Alexander was proud, and it was his pride that led him into the next adventure which he recorded in his autobiography.

He was fourteen at the time, and he was helping with the harvest, standing on the stack in the barnyard, lifting each sheaf on a fork as it was thrown from the loaded cart by the carter. The reapers – called the "shearers" in Lowland dialect – were in the last field of corn, and the master had sent them some bottles of whisky, "partly in honour of it being the last day of shearing, but chiefly to make them drive on at great speed with their work to get it done."

The men carting the corn got none of the whisky and grumbled a good deal. They said to young Sandy Somerville that if they were as clever as he was and could run as fast they would go down to the cornfield and take a bottle. Young Sandy was put on his mettle, and he went. He was seen however by one of the Irish labourers – Michael the laird they called him; and when Alexander had taken his bottle back to the men in the stackyard, Michael the laird purloined two or three for his own use. It was not long before they were missed, and there was an outcry, in which various people were heard saying that "Sandy from the stack-yard done it." Alexander's father was in the cornfield, binding the sheaves as they were cut. He was already angry at the bad, hasty work that was being done because of the whisky, and when he heard that his own son was supposed to have stolen three bottles he strode to the stackyard and thrashed him, telling him he had disgraced himself and the family for ever: the only words he spoke. He burst into tears and went away.

Alexander did not weep. He burned with resentment; to be publicly humiliated, by his own father, and so unjustly! "I resolved to go away and leave home for a long time, and not return until I had lived to be a man, and had done something that would entitle me to respect."

He was not sure where to go. There was his brother James, but he lived too near home. There was another brother, William, who worked in Yorkshire as a forester to the Duke of Devonshire. But he had raised himself in the world, and would, so the boy thought, expect any relation of his to come to him well-dressed, whereas he was only wearing his workaday breeches and nailed boots and highland bonnet. As for the third brother, Peter, he was in the army, and supposed to be at Woolwich which was four hundred miles away, "and I doubted if I would find Peter at Woolwich if I got there; and then I doubted if I should ever find Woolwich."

He spent the night in the stable of the farm where he worked, and at dawn the next morning he left. "The master's riding horse neighed when it heard me moving about the stable; and as I was its groom, in addition to many other offices which I filled on the farm, I opened the corn chest, of which I carried the key, and gave it a feed of corn. It knew me well, and I hung my arms around its neck as it ate the corn, and told it I would never see it more."

"I then took a piece of chalk, and wrote on the top of the corn chest, 'Fare ye well, Branxton, I am away, never to come back.' My heart had been beating all night quick and strong, and my mouth was feverish and thirsty. I went to the pump to have a draught of cold water, and with all seriousness and sorrow, I bade the pump farewell. Coming away from it, my eyes caught sight of my old wheelbarrow on the dunghill, with which I wheeled the clearings from the stables; I turned it upon its feet, lifted it, and put it down again, and said, 'Poor old barrow, I shall never wheel you again.' Coming out of that close, I had to pass the cart in which I had taken the breakfast and dinners, the porridge and bread and beer, so often to the fields to the shearers during that and other harvests. Taking my chalk, I wrote on the bottom of it, 'Parritch cart, I am done with you.' "

Then going up the coach-house lane, between the high holly hedges, he stood a few minutes, wondering which way to go, and wishing that he could take leave of something that belonged to his mother. On an impulse he went up on to the steep hillside, to see if he could find his mother's cow. She was there – Kidley – with the other cows of the village, and he put his arms round her neck and wept while she licked his hand.

One last leave he took of the place where he had grown up. He carved his name on the tree in the Pond Planting, the tree where all his family who had herded cows in those woods had carved the initials of their names. Then he turned his face and his feet towards England. Berwick-upon-Tweed, just over the border, was some twenty-five miles away.

He reached Ayton, where his mother had been born, before eleven o'clock, and wandered into the churchyard. His grandfather was buried there, and two little brothers and a sister. He wondered what they would have been had they lived. Then he stood by the bridge and looked down at the little river where his mother had once washed and bleached clothes and felt more sick at heart about his journey than he had yet been.

"But, I said at last, this is not the way to get on. So I started to the road and reached Berwick, where I spent my penny in the purchase of a loaf, which I ate at about two o'clock, a mile or two from the town on the English side. I had an uncle Peter Orkney in Berwick, and an uncle Alexander Orkney at the Square, two or three miles from that town, both brothers of my mother, and the latter my name-father. I might have just conceived the thought of calling on them, but a glance at my working clothes and nailed boots forbade a repitition of the thought. Besides, they would ask why I had come away from home, and I could not tell that it was because my father gave me a 'licking'; it was the shame I felt at that which had made me leave home.

"After eating my pennyworth of bread – swallowing my all, at once – I proceeded on my journey. I was several miles on the road to Belford, when, being thirsty, I went into one of several poor-looking houses standing in a row by the roadside, and asked a drink of water. A motherly woman took a basin to get me some water, but stopped short of the good errand and asked if I would prefer milk. I said yes, if she pleased. Whereupon she gave me a basin of milk, and bade me sit down and rest if I were tired. I sat down and was drinking the milk, when her husband said, 'Perhaps the lad would like a bit of bread to his milk; do thee, lad?' I was blockhead enough to say, 'No, I thank ye; I am not hungry' – which is considered good manners among young people of my condition in Scotland, no matter how hungry one may be who says so. But the good man of the house said, 'The lad is blate, and wunnot tell; I see he's hungry; give him a piece of bread to the milk.'"

He answered their questions, and the man told him that the farmer there might give him work. But when Alexander had picked his way through a yard terrible with dogs the farmer's wife told him angrily that they had too many idle tramps around, they wanted none of him.

A man whom he overtook on the road gave him shelter for the night in a stable, and then a bowl of porridge in the morning. Alexander told him that he was on his way to Newcastle to go to sea. "Lad," said the man, "ye'll rue that; they'll rope you until thou won't be able to stir thysel. I once went to sea at Newcastle, but I soon ran away again. Go thou home again, lad."

But still Alexander pressed on southward. It was only when he got four miles beyond Belford that he began to consider the matter again. He sat down on the parapet of a bridge and pondered what he was doing. He had no clothes, and no money, but above all he thought of the grief of his mother, "and for the first time since I had left home I prayed to God to direct me what to do, and where to go. I had not so employed my thoughts many minutes, when I felt

assured that it was best to go home. I started at once, my feet going faster than they had gone before, and my thoughts absolutely happy."

"I reached Berwick Bridge without halting, and stood a few

minutes looking over upon the Tweed, and then passed through the town. As soon as I got out of Berwick, I took off my shoes and stockings, and ran bare-footed. Soon after this the Union four-horsed coach came up. It was a fast coach; but so light-footed and light-hearted was I now, that I ran as fast as it. I kept up with it six miles, running about twenty yards behind. The guard once looked back to me, and asked if I had any money. I said 'No,' whereupon he sat down on his seat and did not look at me again. It got away from me at Ayton. I was not able to run up hill with it; but I walked on as fast as I could, and got over the remaining eighteen miles between ten and eleven o'clock at night.

"I did not feel enough of confidence to go to my father's door, but being outrageously hungry, having ate nothing since the crowdy at sunrise, and having walked and run over fifty-two miles of road since then, I was obliged to go to a neighbour's house to get something to eat. Here were two young women, Jean and Alice Dawson, who lived with their blind grandfather, old James Dawson. They rejoiced as much over my return as if they had been my sisters; got out of bed, and made tea for me, and laid me down to sleep; told me how glad

my mother and father, and everyone, would be to know I had returned, and were inquisitive as to where I had been. The distance I had travelled over that day surprised them, as it may do many, considering the want of food, but the number of fifty-two miles is correct, including what I walked in the morning, before I turned."

But he still did not dare go home and lurked at the farm, where the farmer set him to work as though nothing had happened. His mother came and begged him to return, but it was his father that he could not face.

"While I was yet in the straw, in the early morning, my father came to me. He said he had been lying awake all the night, and nearly the whole of every night I had been away, and so had my poor mother. With his eyes wet, and the tears running down his venerable face, he asked me to forgive him for the wrong he had done; for he had since found that the men sent me to take the whisky for their use, and that they drank it. For me to be begged of for forgiveness by my father! It was worse – aye, far more painful – than the hasty punishment was which he inflicted on me. I never again saw him raise his hand in punishment or rebuke; and, so far as I can remember, he never again spoke a severe word to me."

The NAVIGATOR, with pickaxe and spade,
Who works very hard till a railway is made.

'Dandy Dick'

THE YOUNG NAVVY

IN 1835 a boy ran away from the remote Hertfordshire village where he lived, because he wanted to build railways. His name is now lost. We only know that the navvies called him "Dandy Dick", so that it is probable his first name was Richard. It was a time when railways were the most sensational new thing there was, though there were plenty of people strongly prejudiced against them. Certainly the boy's guardian had told him to drop the idea at once.

He was sixteen when he announced his ambition. He could not keep away from railways. In his last autumn term at a school near Harrow he used to climb over the playground wall and run away to watch a stretch of the London and Birmingham line being built. Wild with enthusiasm, he bought himself Grier's *Mechanic's Calculator* and Jones' *Levelling* and taught himself to work out gradients and calculate earthworks.

"I left school resolved to be an engineer. My guardian was equally resolved that I should not have my own way in the matter; so I rose early one morning in the month of March, eighteen hundred and thirty-five, packed up a change of linen and an extra pair of trousers, with my Grier in a handkerchief, and with but a few shillings in my pocket, set off for the nearest railway works. There I hoped to obtain employment, and, by beginning at the beginning, to follow upon their own road the Smeatons, Stephensons, and Brunels."

Twenty years later, in an anonymous article contributed to *Household Words*, he set down his memories of those railway pioneering days. He called the article *Navvies as They Used to Be*, and emphasized how things had changed since the 1830's. Navvies then were wild lawless armies who settled in crude shanty towns which they built themselves near the workings. "These banditti," a railway engineer had called them, "the terror of the surrounding countryside." They plundered, murdered, and rioted; they also died violent deaths in the course of their work – the boy saw it all and managed to survive. It was a savage age, when lives were held cheap, when there was little in the way of a police force, and little concern for the conditions in which anybody lived or worked.

For those days, navvies earned good wages; three times, perhaps what a farm labourer might get. They were skilled men doing a dangerous job. They followed a contractor round from one railway working to another until he had no more work on hand, and then off they tramped to find it elsewhere. They did the work for which an experienced touch was needed, like blasting and cutting, bridge- and tunnel-building, masonry; leaving the drudgery such as filling and tipping the trucks of earth from the diggings, to boys and unskilled locals.

So when our boy arrived at Boxmoor thirty miles from his home where they were building the London to Birmingham railway (the same line that he had watched from school) they took him on without asking any awkward questions, at a weekly wage of twelve shillings. His job was to drive a horse and truck full of earth along the temporary rails of the embankment that was being built, and tip it at the end. The navvies were amused, and told him he "looked too much like a ha'porth of soap after a hard day's wash to be fit for much," but they left him alone until in his third week he tipped, not just the earth, but the horse and the cart over the edge of the embankment.

He lost his wages, and his job, and tramped off to find another. That same evening he arrived at Watford tunnel, and there he hired himself to a foul-mouthed Yorkshire sub-contractor called Frazer.

"My job under this man was bucket-steering. Placed upon the projecting ledge of a scaffold some eighty feet above the level of the rails in the tunnel, and one or two hundred feet below the surface of the earth, while bricklayers, masons, and labourers were busy upon the brickwork of the shaft above, below and round me, while

YOUNG SIXFOOT

& WHAT BECAME OF HIM.

By Mrs CHARLES GARNET.

Society for Promoting Christian Knowledge,
NORTHUMBERLAND AVENUE, LONDON.

torches and huge fires in cressets were blazing everywhere, I was, in the midst of the din and smoke, to steer clear of the scaffold the descending earth-buckets, one of which dropped under my notice every three minutes at the least. This duty demanding vigilant attention, I had to perform for an unbroken shift (as it was termed) of six hours at a stretch.

" 'Look thou,' said Frazer with an oath, 'you just do like this.' I was to clasp a pole with my left arm, hang over the abyss, and steady the buckets with a stick held out in my right hand.

" 'Do like this,' he repeated, swearing, 'but mind, if you fall, go clean down without doing any mischief. Last night I'd to pay for a new trowel that the little fool who was killed yesterday knocked out of a fellow's hand.' The little fool was the poor lad whom I replaced, and as I afterwards learned, was a runaway watchmaker's apprentice out of Coventry, who had been worked for three successive shifts without relief, and who had fallen down the shaft from sheer exhaustion. And before I knocked off my first shift, I was not surprised at his fate. I was so thoroughly exhausted that Frazer put me into the bucket, and gave orders to a man to bear a hand with me to Sanders's fuddling crib, and let me have a pitch in for an hour, and a pint."

The fuddling crib was a hut near the bottom of the shaft, and the pitch in was a mattress. There were several mattresses on which were sprawled men and boys all in a state of complete exhaustion. Our boy slept for six hours, and as soon as he opened his eyes he was thrown off the mattress to make room for the next sleeper, and sent to the drinking den next door to get his pint. He swopped this for some coffee, but he never got it to his lips because it was knocked out of his hand by a giant of a man who rushed past shouting "Hist! hist! Red Whipper's a gwain to fight the devil!"

"I looked round. Seated on one of the benches about half way down the hut was a man who had fallen asleep over his beer. He wore a loose red serge frock and red night-cap, the peak of which appeared through a newspaper which had been thrust over his head, and hung down to his knees. A momentary hush prevailed; when the man who had knocked down my coffee, returning with a light, set fire to the paper. Red Whipper was instantly enveloped in flame,

WORKING-SHAFT.-KILSBY TUNNEL. July 8th 1837.

and started from his sleep in fierce alarm, throwing his arms about him like a madman. This joke was called fighting the devil."

The boy preferred the turmoil in the tunnel to the drunken scuffling in the hut. He left a vivid description of that scene, hundreds of feet below ground.

"There was no day there, and no peace; the shrill roar of escaping steam; the groans of mighty engines heaving ponderous loads of earth to the surface; the click-clack of lesser engines pumping dry the numerous springs by which the drift was intersected; the reverberating thunder of the small blasts of powder fired upon the mining works; the rumble of trains of trucks; the clatter of horses' feet; the clank of chains . . . There were to be seen miners from Cornwall, drift-borers from Wales, pitmen from Staffordshire and Northumberland, engineers from Yorkshire and Lancashire, navvies – Englishmen, Scotchmen, and Irishmen – from everywhere, muck-shifters, pickmen, barrowmen, brakesmen, banksmen, drivers, gaffers, gangers, carpenters, bricklayers, labourers, and boys of all sorts, ages and sizes; some engaged upon the inverts beneath the rails, some upon the drains below these, some upon the extension of the drifts, some clearing away the falling earth, some loading it upon the trucks, some working like bees in cells building up the tunnel sides, some upon the centre turning the great arches, some stretched upon their backs putting the key-bricks to the crown – all speaking in a hundred dialects, with dangers known and unknown impending on every side; with commands and countermands echoing about through air murky with the smoke and flame of burning tar-barrels, cressets, and torches.''

With the fuddling shops there below ground, and men blind drunk or blind with exhaustion there were accidents of course. There was a terrible disaster a few months after the boy arrived. Nobody could be certain what caused it, but he thought that a drunken bricklayer had taken out the centring under a newly-built arch, for the tunnel caved in, burying thirty men. It was a fearful scene. Above, in the woods above the tunnel, was a huge abyss into which whole trees had been sucked, and thousands of tons of earth had poured down it into the workings below. Fourteen men died, and the body of the last one was not found until the navvies had dug for three weeks.

There was a similar sort of accident at the second tunnel where the boy worked, Northchurch tunnel. Here the tunnel diggers struck a vein of sand in the roof. Just one blow of a pickaxe, and the sand began to pour down, running like water. The foreman knew the danger – that the earth above, no longer supported by the vein of sand, would crash down into the tunnel – and the gang made frenzied efforts to shore up the roof before it was too late. There was a low rumbling like distant guns, then thundering crashes, and while the men were rushing away the whole mass of earth, masonry, timber and sand collapsed upon them. Five men were buried, three were dug out alive and taken off to the infirmary.

But there were sights more horrifying than the mangled bodies. Funerals were popular social functions among navvies, and on this occasion the overseer of the dead men's gang, a man by the name of Hicks, was elated at the prospect of all the randy boozing that lay ahead. He got up a subscription, a shilling a head from all the gangs in the tunnel. It came to twenty pounds. Five pounds of it were put aside to bury the dead, the rest was to go in drink.

"The funerals took place on the afternoon of the Sunday following the disaster, in the churchyard of Northchurch parish. The procession was headed by Hicks, who walked before the coffins; behind followed about fifty navvies, all more or less drunk, and the rear was brought up by a host of stragglers, and country girls, the companions of the navvies. There were no real mourners; the unfortunate men being strangers in the district, and the residences of their friends unknown.

"It was about half-past two o'clock when the train reached the gates of the churchyard. At the church-door the officiating minister, observing the condition of the men, wisely ordered the church to be closed, and proceeded to lead the way to the grave. Hicks took umbrage at this, and threatened to break the door open; but as this was not seconded among his men, he told them to put the coffins on the ground, and let the parson do all the business himself. But the men hesitated, the sexton protested, and at length the grave was reached.

"Here Hicks found fresh cause for offence. It was a single grave and he said (which was untrue) that separate graves had been paid for. When this was disproved, he objected that the one grave was not deep enough, and ordered two of his men to jump in and dig it to Hell. The men jumped in as ordered, one had the sexton's pickaxe, the other the spade, and in little more than ten minutes the grave was ten feet deeper. Still the men dug on, and continued their labour, till they could no longer throw the earth to the surface. Then rose the question, how were they to get out? The sexton's short ladder was useless, for the grave was at least twenty feet deep. Hicks settled the matter by calling for 'the ropes!' 'What ropes?' 'The coffin ropes.' These were brought and lowered to the men. With a loud hurrah they were drawn up, and the clergyman was told to 'go on'.

"The good man, pale and terrified, incoherently hurried through the service, closed the book, and was gathering up his surplice for a precipitate departure, when Hicks grasped him by the collar and, with fearful imprecations, demanded a gallon or two of beer, 'for' he said, 'you do not get two of 'em in the hole every day.' Then followed an atrocious scene. A crowd had collected in the church-yard, and several of the villagers came forth to the rescue of their curate, who narrowly escaped uninjured. A desperate fight, during which one or two men were thrown into the open grave, terminated the affair."

Hicks and his navvies drank their way through the funeral money from Sunday till Tuesday, when they were arrested, blind drunk, and thrown into prison. But this did not stop the men's enthusiasm for a funeral blow-out. Shortly after Christmas, when another man was killed, his ganger suggested raffling the body. The idea was very well received, and nearly three hundred men joined the scheme. The raffle money, sixpence a head, was to go towards funeral drink, and the funeral was to be paid for by those who drew the highest and the lowest numbers. The body was raffled, but nobody would pay for the funeral, so the dead man was eventually given a pauper's burial by the parish.

Drinking and brawling – this was how the navvy spent his free time. Any excuse would serve. Fighting in gangs, Scots against Irish, navvies against police, was most to their taste, and the newspapers of the 1830's used to be full of headlines like "desperate affray with navigators" or "fearful battle between navigators and the police". But sometimes they fought single-handed. The boy remembered a "purring-match" between two men from Wigan who quarrelled about some detail in their work. "Send for the purring-boots!" their mates shouted, and everybody jumped down from the scaffolding and made for the fields nearby.

"The purring-boots duly came. They were stout high-lows, each shod with an iron-plate, standing an inch or so in advance of the toe. Each man was to wear one boot, with which he was to kick the other to the utmost. A toss took place for right or left, and the winner of the right having a small foot the boot was stuffed with hay to make it fit. I refrain from particulars: I have said enough to show the brutal nature of the affray. It lasted more than an hour. The victor was a pitiable object for months, and his foe was crippled for life."

The fight was the important thing, any excuse would do. The boy remembered a fearful one between two platelayers about whether the word "beetle" or "mawl" was the right one for a certain tool.

To a certain extent he was protected against the worst of navvy life. He found a friend, Canting George, "a tall, thin, hard-lined, stern-featured, middle-aged man, commonly sneered at by his fellows because he was said to be religious; though I never knew him attempt to make a proselyte, or interfere at any time by word or deed with drinking, swearing, quarrelling, or fighting. His only cause of offence was that he was never at any time drunk or riotous himself. Canting George was a native of an obscure spot in Warwickshire. He was an extreme Calvinist, and miserably ignorant, for he could not even read; yet he possessed very good reasoning powers."

Canting George attached himself to the boy and shielded him from some of the violence of Happy Jack, Long Bob, Dusty Tom, Billy Goat, Frying Dan, Red Head, and other members of the gang of forty. Navvies always used nicknames, nothing else, and the boy was known as Dandy Dick because of his new clothes and tools. If it had not been for George standing up for him, the boy would have been dragged from his respectable lodgings and forced to live in a

s the careful POLICEMAN, who stands,
'o guard us from danger, with flag in his hands.

s the QUEEN, who oft goes by the train,
ןnd Windsor receives her at home once again.

s the RAIL, which for miles is laid down,
ןnd takes you, by steam, such a long way from
town.

shanty with the rest of the gang "and rather than have done that, I should have given up the effort to make myself an engineer altogether."

The shanty was a building of stone, brick, mud, and timber with a roof of tile and tarpaulin. Like other navvy shanties, it had been hastily thrown together so the men could doss down as close to their work as possible. "There were several of these dens of wild men round about the works. The bricklayers, masons, mechanics, and their labourers were distributed among the adjacent population, carrying disorder and uproar wherever they went." The shanties each had a housekeeper, a blear-eyed crone, who made the beds and washed and cooked, and got mauled by the navvies in fights, and beaten by them when they were drunk.

"Once only I visited our shanty. I was, in spare hours, teaching George to read; and it happened one Sunday morning early in May that the rain hindering church attendance, I strolled up to the shanty to find George; but he was gone out. Old Peg, the presiding crone, who was then exhibiting two black eyes and a bandaged chin, told me that he would be back by eleven, and having cursed me in a way intended to be very friendly, she invited me to wait till he returned. So I sat down on a three-legged stool, and took a survey of the place.

"The door was about midway in one of the sides, having a window on each side of it, and near one of the windows were a few rude benches and seats. Of such of my comrades as were up, four or five were sprawling on these seats, two lying flat upon the earthen floor playing at cards, and one sat on a stool mending his boots. These men all greeted me with a gruff welcome, and pressed me to drink. Near the other window were three barrels of beer, all in tap, the keys of which were chained to a stout leathern girdle, which encircled old Peg's waist. Her seat – an old-fashioned arm-chair – was handy to these barrels, of which she was tapster. The opposite side and one end of the building were fitted up from floor to roof – which was low – in a manner similar to the between-decks of an emigrant ship. In each of the berths lay one or two of my mates – for this was their knock-off Sunday – all drunk or asleep. Each man lay with his head upon his ket (his bundle of clothes); and nestling with many of the men were dogs and litters of puppies of the bull or lurcher breed; for a navvy's dog was, of course, either for fighting or poaching.

"The other end of the room served as the kitchen. There was a rude dresser in one corner, upon which and a ricketty table was arranged a very miscellaneous set of plates and dishes, in tin, wood, and earthenware, each holding an equally ill-matched cup, basin, or bowl. Against the wall were fixed a double row of cupboards or lockers, one to each man. Over the fireplace, which was nearly central, there were also hung about a dozen guns. In the other corner was a large copper, beneath which a blazing fire was roaring; a volume of savoury steam was escaping from beneath the lid, and old Peg, muttering and spluttering ever and anon, threw on more coals and kept the copper boiling."

Strings came out of the copper, each with a bit of wood on the end, and these, old Peg explained, were tied on to the men's bits of dinner, all simmering away in the pot. One had a bit of beef, another had just potatoes, Billy Goat had cabbage and bacon, and Red Whipper had a leveret – twenty separate dinners each in its own net.

Soon after the boy's visit to his gang's shanty there was a bloody affray with another gang in a shanty opposite. It took place two hours after pay-time, when the men had already drunk enough to make them fighting mad. It lasted for an hour. Picks, spades, shovels, mawls – they seized everything that was lying around. His gang won, five of them wounded to twelve badly mangled Irishmen in the other gang. The Irishmen's shanty was burnt to the ground, and the whole affair was held to be thoroughly satisfying.

By 1836 the navvies' way of life had become such a scandal that it was generally agreed something must be done. The first efforts to reclaim them were made by religious missions. Well-meaning people came out to the railway workings to harangue the men while they sprawled over their food in the meal-breaks. Red Whipper and Billy Goat and their mates did not take kindly to this sort of thing. The boy met a missionary who confided to him all the cruel tricks that had been played on him, how he had been sent out to the edge of the tip in trucks, deposited on the spoil heap, and dangled down the tunnel shaft in a bucket. Another man who was very officious in the distribution of tracts found they were all being used to paper the shanties.

It was the action of the contractors that at last civilized the armies who worked for them. Men like Peto, Brassey, and Jackson saw to it that decent housing was provided. They stopped the gangers from keeping beer-shops, and forbade beer to be brought to the workings. Working hours were regulated, pay was given in money, not beer and provisions; men no longer worked fuddled with drink and fatigue. Twenty years more and the navvy was transformed in the minds of the British public. He was no longer a bloodthirsty brute who terrorized the district unlucky enough to have railway workings; he was the salt of the earth, the honest English labourer, the hero of the Crimean War, the man who was sent for by contractors up and down Europe who could not build their railways without the English working man.

Is the **MILE-MARK**, that never is wrong,
And shows us how quickly the train goes along.

Charles

RIOTS AND THE WORKHOUSE

"I WONDER whether it is true that I was allowed to be worked for fourteen hours a day when a little over seven years of age," wrote Charles Shaw, contrasting the plenty that he saw about him in 1893 with the famine and despair of the Pottery towns in the Hungry Forties. "Whether it is true that even poor children now receive a better education than what I heard 'Tom Hughes'* once say he received when a boy at a much greater cost? I wonder whether it is true that I ate the sparse and miserably adulterated bread of the Corn Law times; if the rags, and squalor, and severe labour and long hours of those days, as contrasted with the leisure, and plenty, and recreation of these days are all illusions? I wonder if these are real people in their thronging thousands, on holiday, that I see, who have shares in 'stores', who have deposits in the savings banks, who have portmanteaux, boxes of all sizes and kinds, making up tons of

* Thomas Hughes, the author of *Tom Brown's Schooldays* (1857).

baggage in connection with a trip, surpassing that of 'their betters' seventy years ago?''

Of course poverty could still be found in plenty in the 1890's, but not the complete destitution that turned men into savage packs of wolves. Take strikes, for instance. In his childhood these meant that the strikers' families starved, and the men, maddened with despair would run amok; smashing, killing. In the strike that he was experiencing as he wrote in the '90's so much money had been contributed to the relief of the needy that there were very few cases of real suffering.

To Charles Shaw, when he set down his memories of childhood, the Hungry Forties seemed – from the distance of half a century – something unreal. It was the same when as a boy he used to look at pottery figures of Napoleon. The small factory where he and his father worked used to turn them out in thousands; Napoleon had become a pretty ornament, much in demand, painted in dark blue and buff and gold. But he had been an ogre and a demon to the English people of thirty years before. "It is difficult in these days to realize how the terror of Napoleon had saturated the minds of the lower classes in England. Yet, as I looked at the figure, it only then represented a figure.''

So the Hungry Forties had become only a name; the suffering had passed; a new generation was incredulous when grandparents remembered the pale hollow faces of the poor who stood silently in the market-place at Tunstall, waiting for the dole of coal and bread to be distributed. The cold was ferocious, men had been turned off work, there was no food, no warmth in the houses, and the parish poor law guardians had had to take special measures to keep the people alive. "The crowd in the market-place on such a day formed a ghastly sight. Pinched faces of men, with a stern, cold silence of manner. Moaning women, with crying children in their arms. Twenty people of any other time would have made more noise than this hungry crowd did." Fifty years later, Charles Shaw still remembered with loathing the taste of that Poor Law bread, which seemed to be made of ground straw, alum, and plaster of Paris.

It was not just the Potteries; in 1842 the poor in England touched perhaps their lowest point in want and misery. It was the good old days, said' Charles Shaw bitterly, when the Corn Laws made rent high and living low, and made semi-famine the ordinary condition of the toiling masses. "Pinched faces and shivering bodies were seen everywhere during that cruel winter, carts were followed for miles for any coal they might lose on their journeys, and a jolt was a godsend to the eager follower at the cart tail. The glistening lumps as they fell made eyes glisten, as it meant fire in the black shining treasure. Shord-rucks* were searched by shivering women and children for cinders, as hens scratch and search for food. Fingers bled as they picked in among the broken pitchers and shords, and the bleeding was only staunched by dirt and frost."

The poor rioted that year, it was one of Charles Shaw's most vivid and dread memories. The Pottery towns, like other manufacturing districts up and down the country, were seething with tumult. They had expected great things of the Reform Bill ten years before, but it had given them no more food, it only seemed to have made the middle classes more powerful. The People's Charter was their hope

* Pottery spoil-heaps.

ATTACK ON THE WORKHOUSE AT STOCKPORT.

now, and Chartist meetings inflamed them. Speakers told them that the people must have power, and that if they loyally supported Chartism they would tumble the tyrants in the dust.

In July, 1842 there was a colliers' strike. Lack of coal meant that many of the pot-works had to close, and the misery in the Pottery towns was intensified. On 15 August a huge crowd listened to one of their number denouncing the people's oppressors, and were stirred into a frenzy of violence. They broke into buildings, wrecked, plundered, drank themselves into even greater frenzy, and went on to more pillage and destruction. Next morning they marched on Burslem, thousands strong, singing the Chartist hymn:

> The lion of freedom's let loose from his den,
> And we'll rally around him again and again.

At Burslem they were joined by a throng of half-dressed, half-starved weavers, armed with sticks and stones, and here in the Swan Square they were confronted by a magistrate and a troop of soldiers behind him. "What do you want?" he asked them and they shouted back: "Our rights and liberties, the Charter, and more to eat." Sticks and stones were thrown, and then the soldiers fired.

The panic, the chaos and the injuries in that square packed with people were long remembered in the Potteries. Charles himself did not see the soldiers charge, but he heard the rattle of muskets, and ran from the field where he was playing. He met the wounded people streaming out of the town, as if they were pursued by wild beasts. There was a cobbler whom he knew, with the crown cut off his hat, and the bridge of his nose slit in two, telling the people round him how the soldiers had tried to cut off his head. Charles pressed on to the market place. Here the soldiers were trying to drive the sullen, slow-moving crowds away, but streams of people were pouring in. When the cavalry began to clear the narrow streets the confusion, groans and shrieks were terrible, so was the agony of fear on the faces of the men and women. When they managed to escape outside the town, said Shaw, "they halted in broken groups to tell of escapes and sufferings. In want, in terror, and with a sense of the crushing injustice of the times, they cursed the land in which they had been born."

And again Shaw blessed the times he was now living in that such savagery belonged to the past. The towns in the '40's might have been surrounded by fields and country lanes, but social conditions were unspeakably worse. He remembered a little valley on the western side of Tunstall, the town where he was born, where he fished in the stream and picked buttercups and daisies and lady's smock. Chatterly Farm, which supplied the milk for the town, lay in these fields. By the 1890's this peaceful valley was choked with smoke and disfigured by mounds of slag and dirt from the mines. Where birds once sang in the woods railway engines now snorted and blew, and trucks jangled. The farm buildings stood blasted and desolate. But there was prosperity in the town now, and nobody starved.

Overcrowding, gin palaces, drunkenness: you could certainly find all these in the towns of the '90's, but the people had some money in their pockets, and the sad old square where the dole of parish bread had been given out had changed into a busy covered market where the people jostled each other happily to buy what had been unobtainable luxuries before.

Nor did birds in the woods outside and leafy country lanes mean that the towns of the old days were pleasant places. The Pottery towns as he remembered them were a hideous, unplanned sprawl of dilapidated cottages, broken pavements, rutted tracks, open drains, and small ramshackle manufactories which were often nothing more than a collection of tumble-down hovels set up by anybody who had a few pounds in his pocket and wanted to be a master potter on his own account. Such for instance was the manufactory where Charles and his father went to paint the figures of Napoleon. But though Charles was hardly more than a child when he went there, it was in fact his third job, and by far his happiest.

He says very little about his home life – perhaps because, poor child, he was allowed to spend so few hours of the day at home. From the age of seven he was working for fourteen hours daily, and was out of the house from five in the morning till past nine at night, six days a week. His grandfather – though Charles did not discover this until he was a grown man – had been a prosperous dealer in china and earthenware "who had commanded more ready money than any man in the Potteries". The business had been wrecked by one of the sons, and Charles' own father had been employed as a painter and gilder in the Davenport china manufactory. Painters and gilders were highly skilled workers, the aristocrats of the industry, but Charles' father fell foul of the manager, supported a strike against him and was ruined by him. Charles could hardly remember a time when the furniture was not disappearing out of the house piece by piece each week to feed the family. Even so, he came home on many Saturday nights to find there was not a morsel of food in the house, and the next day, Sunday, to be lived through somehow.

At the age of seven he had been taken away from the little dame school where he had learned his letters since he was three. A kind-hearted neighbour saw the distress that the family was in, and suggested that he should work for her son Jack as a mould-runner. He could earn a shilling a week this way, and it would provide a little food.

Jack moulded plates in a pot-works. As mould-runner Charles' job was to take the soft clay plates into the stove-room to dry out, and stack them on the shelves round the red-hot stove. As the lower shelves got filled he had to climb up step-ladders to reach the higher ones. When the wet clay had dried, the plates came back to the "master" to be tooled and smoothed, then back they went to the stove room again for further drying. All this had to be done at the double, otherwise the boy was cursed and belted. In between the running he had to prepare the clay, hammering and thumping it into a putty-like consistency – work that is now done by hydraulic presses. He also had to get to work early enough to light the fire in the stove before Jack came, and this meant, since fire-making materials were not provided, raiding one of the ovens where pottery

was firing, and carrying off hot coals on a shovel pursued by an angry fireman.

The potteries were one of the last industries to organize themselves properly. Few employers supervised their workers or concerned themselves with the brutality and violence in the workshops. As long as the output was maintained the men could do what they liked, farm out their work, drink themselves stupid, seduce the women, and drive the boys till they dropped. And they did nothing whatever to stop the men keeping Monday and sometimes Tuesday as an unofficial holiday. Saint Monday, Charles Shaw called it, and said repeatedly what an evil practice it was.

He first came across it when he was eight. He had changed his job of a mould-runner to make cup and mug handles at another pot-works. He soon found that though he was required to be at the "pot-bank" (as the works were called) six days a week, he was not needed on Monday until breakfast-time, and that the works had a holiday look on Monday and Tuesday. This was because most of the men were away drinking while the women and the boys loafed around the workshops. They might drink too, perhaps spend all night on the premises – there was nobody to care what they did.

Then, from Wednesday to Saturday the men worked like galley-slaves to get the week's work finished, and saw to it that the women and boys did too. Charles remembered after a fourteen or fifteen hour day being almost too tired to walk the mile and a half home. He had had his dinner of bread and butter at one o'clock and after that there would be nothing to eat until he got home at nine or ten. His mother would spoon a bit of porridge into his mouth, put him to bed and then get him up again at four in the morning. "The poor child never sees his parents after Monday night except at this weary meal, for four days a week, and a few minutes every morning."

The "masters" might drink away Monday and Tuesday at the Foaming Quart beer-house over the road, but the boys were supposed to be preparing their cup handles unsupervised. Of course they larked instead, and equally inevitably they got flogged for it when the men came in to work on Wednesday. A rope an inch thick and clogged with clay was used for the purpose. "The man in his wild passion laid this with all his might upon the back of the poor little handle-maker. In spite of yells and screams and cries for mercy on the part of the boy, and in spite of the entreaties of those who looked on, the blows fell thick and fast. I have seen when the shirt was forced into the boy's flesh, and after being dried in during the day's work, it has had to be sponged with warm water so as to get it out of the bruises."

Charles himself, terrified of a flogging, tried to run away one Tuesday night. He had not made the number of cup handles demanded for Wednesday, and he knew that if he went home he would be made to go to work as usual the next day. So he skulked around the outlying brickfields, looking for somewhere he could sleep. The dark terrified him, but at last he thought of the ovens at the tileworks where he might be allowed to warm himself. "The ovenmen, I knew, if somewhat rough, were kind-hearted men. Many outcasts and wanderers in those days, before casual wards came into existence, were sheltered at those ovens. I was received there with a kindly welcome and given a drink of buttermilk. I was told to sit down in a little shelter opposite an oven mouth, and after my little story was told, I was left alone." The tilemakers took him back to work next morning and either threatened or pleaded with the "master". At any rate, Charles was not flogged that time.

Sometimes the handlemakers were told to get to work by three o'clock so that the "masters" could finish their week's quota. The

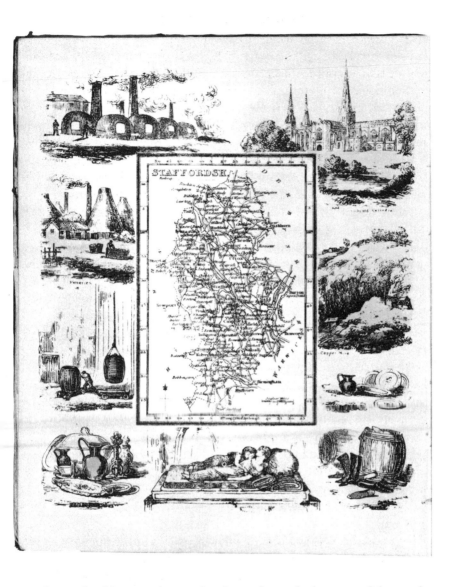

watchman had instructions to let them through the gate of the works at that time.

"Poor Bill S. and I wended our way home one night between nine and ten o'clock. Bill had been so often punished that he was full of fear on this particular occasion. We parted with the understanding that he was to call for me about half-past two in the morning, as he had to pass our door.

"As I was so often woke up when drenched with uneasiness, I was not surprised when told Bill S. had called for me. I was told further that it could not be the time Bill said it was, but as we had neither clock nor watch in the house, and poor Bill's fears made him urgent, we started. When we got near the turnpike, we met some nightsoil men* with their 'tumbrils' and when we asked them the time, they laughingly told us it was only just turned half-past twelve. With weary steps we toiled on to Burslem, and stood opposite the Town Hall clock just as it struck one. What could we do? We had seen a little old cobbler near the works, going into his cottage, as we passed, evidently just before going to bed, and we durst not go back and ask him to let us in. We durst not go to the works, for the watch-man always had with him a big dog, and to mount the gate with such a terror before us was out of the question. So we stood looking at the clock under the window of an inn opposite for a whole hour; then, at two o'clock, we decided to go to call up another lad who had to be at work at the same time as ourselves. We sheltered in his home for half an hour, and then went to the works, and found the watchman and Turk, the dog, ready to receive us.

"Perhaps about this time the statesmen in London were going to their luxurious coaches, thinking of the greatness and glory and freedom of England, and thanking God we were not as other nations. We lit our farthing candles, and soon our handle moulds were rattling like dancing dolls. And yet these little white slaves were flogged at times nearly as brutally, all things considered, as Legree flogged Uncle Tom. Nearly all England wept about thirteen years later for Uncle Tom, but no fine lady or gentleman wept for the cruelly-used pottery children."

Cruel as life was for these children, they would all have rather made their handles in the noisome underground pits at the pot-bank, however savage their master, than endure the work-house. This was the next stage in Charles Shaw's childhood; he and a younger brother and a baby sister, together with his parents, had to "go to Chell."

"I had heard that phrase before. It was often used in those days in bitterness and contempt and loathing. I have often wondered if the

---

* Employed to empty the cess-pits.

word carries to other ears, and in these later days, all the inward repulsiveness of the words 'poorhouse' and 'bastille.' Chell, Chell, Chell, was ever in those days a cruel word, with a metallic harshness in its utterance. The district was pleasant and healthy, with green fields stretching far away, and yet there was a building upon it which cast a blighting shadow – from the poverty, the suffering, and the harshness it symbolised."

There had been a change in the attitude to the poor since John Shipp's childhood. The poorhouse had offered scanty comfort then, certainly, but it was not held to be such an abject disgrace to be in it. Since then opinion had hardened against the poor, and to try to shed themselves of the numbers who depended upon the poor rates, the authorities had since 1834 decreed that those who could not support themselves outside must be shut up inside high walls and treated with the utmost severity. Mary Howitt in middle age felt sadly how things had changed for the worse since her childhood.

Charles had to accompany his family to Chell because he was too young to be left outside, as his older brothers were, to fend for him-

ON THEIR WAY TO THE WORKHOUSE

self. But for the first time his work had become almost pleasant. He had been moved from the "pot-bank" to the part of the works where chinaware was manufactured. Here the atmosphere was far soberer; there was no drinking, no rowdyism, and "Old Rupert", the handler he worked for, was kind and considerate. Not only did he share his food with Charles, who was often sent to work without any, but he gave him a holiday from time to time and took him out in the country. But now, one morning in the late autumn of 1842, without a chance to say goodbye to "Old Rupert", he was taken to the workhouse.

"Early in the morning we left a home without a morsel of food. We called on a relative who had kindly provided breakfast for us, and yet it was a wretched meal for my parents. I remember how the food seemed to choke as much as the sobs, and the vain entreaties to 'eat a little more'. We went by the field road to Chell, so as to escape as much observation as possible. One child had to be carried as she was too young to walk. . . .

"And so we came to our big home for the time. The very vastness of it chilled us. Our reception was more chilling still. Everybody we saw and spoke to looked metallic, as if worked from within by a hidden machinery. Their voices were metallic, and sounded harsh and imperative. The younger ones huddled more closely to their parents, as if from fear of these stern officials. Doors were unlocked by keys belonging to bunches, and the sound of keys and locks and bars, and doors banging, froze the blood within us. We finally landed in a cellar, clean and bare, and as grim as I have since seen in prison cells. We were told this was the place where we should have to be washed and put on our workhouse attire. Nobody asked us if we were tired, or if we had had any breakfast. We might have committed some unnameable crime, or carried some dreaded infection."

The children were roughly undressed, washed in cold water, and put into harsh textured clothes, which were covered up by a pinafore. Then they were dragged screaming from their parents, who were separated too. Charles was put in the charge of the schoolmaster, and shoved into a large room which served both as dining room and schoolroom. The lessons he could manage well enough; he had learned to read and write at the dame school. But the food even he,

POOR LAW IMPRISONMENT. — THE UNION WINDOWS ALWAYS LOOKING INWARDS, COUNTRY PROSPECTS
ARE EXCHANGED FOR EXPANSIVE VIEWS OF THE WALLS. WOMEN'S ROOM AT THE WORKHOUSE

used to the poorest and scantiest meals, found repulsive: greasy
water with lumps of gristle in it that needed a tiger's teeth to break.
This was dinner. For the evening meal they were brought a hunk of
bread and a jug of skilly. Workhouse skilly was known the breadth
of England as the most nauseating compound of oatmeal and water
ever laid before humans, sour, mouldy, filthy. Long after workhouses such as Chell had been replaced by more humane institutions
"skilly" was remembered with loathing. "It might have been boiled
in old clothes," said Charles Shaw of his first experience of it, "old
clothes which had been worn upon sweating bodies for three-score
years and ten."

But the food was nothing compared to the ordeal of night in the
dormitory with little savages who bullied and terrorized the weaker
boys into agonies of fear. They told them stories of ghosts and
murders, they waylaid the ones who visited the tub at the top of the
stairs. (There was no sanitation in the workhouses of those days,
and in the morning the tub would have to be carried downstairs to
be emptied, slopping lavishly over the floor as it went). "Misfortune
brought boys there who shrank to the very narrow of their souls from
the brutalities, obscenities and coarseness allowed. Other boys were

verily 'children of the devil'; yet these two sorts of boys were forced into association and community."*

Sunday was a blessed interlude, even though the terrors of the night were not abated. For one thing there was a thin slice of cheese to eat with the dinner bread. Before they could eat it they had to listen, standing, to a long sermon from the clergyman who had just given them a sermon in church. But when it was over, and the clergyman departed, nobody could have relished a sumptuous dinner more "than we did that bit of cheese. It was the one bit of food that reminded us of home."

And then, on Sunday afternoon, the children who had mothers were allowed to go to the women's room. "It was an oasis in the desert of our common life. The Sunday afternoon shone through all the week. Even the troubles which burdened the children's hearts got release on the Sunday. Many stories of young griefs were told in the mother's ear, but forgotten as soon as told. There was, however, one dreadful moment, when the bell was rung in the room by a porter to tell us our time was gone. We knew that he would let us have no supper that night if we did not leave the room at once."

The workhouse did not mean an escape from the sort of flogging that most boys had to endure at work. Far from it; most of them were beaten or cuffed in the ordinary course of the day. But during the time that Charles was at Chell there was one special flogging, that made a deep impression on him.

The boy concerned was always in trouble; he was energetic and lively and the authorities thought he must be subdued. Constant punishment made him reckless and defiant, and one day he had had enough of it; he ran away, and was, of course, recaptured, within a few hours.

"This incident made an awful flutter in our little dove-cote. All sorts of punishment were imagined as likely to be inflicted, but the boys who had been longest in the workhouse said he would be flogged in the presence of the other boys with a pickled birch rod – that is a rod which has been kept soaking in salt water. After the usual skilly

* Though Charles Shaw in his indignation thought that conditions like these could only be found in workhouses, the dormitories of the English public schools of the time were often quite as bad. There are appalling accounts of the depravity and violence among the Scholars at Eton. See Arthur Duke Coleridge: *Eton in the Forties*, 1896.

supper that night we were all told to remain in the room. None were to go out on any account. The long table was cleared, and a smaller square table was brought in and placed in the middle of the room. The knowing ones whispered that the flogging would take place on this table.

"Several persons came in whom we did not usually see. Then the governor came in. We were duly informed by him what was to take place, the bad qualities of the runaway were ponderously and slowly described, and we were exhorted in menacing tones to take warning by his 'awful example'.

"When the solemn harangue was finished, the poor boy was pushed into the room like a sheep for the slaughter. He had a wild, eager look. His eyes flashed, and searched the room and all present with rapid glances. His body was stripped down to his waist, and in the yellow and sickly candlelight of the room his heart could be seen beating against his poor thin ribs. The boy was lifted on to the table, and four of the biggest boys were called out to hold each a leg or an arm. . . .

"How long the flogging went on, I cannot say, but screaming became less and less piercing, and at last the boy was taken out, giving vent only to heavy sobs at intervals. How that poor little wretch got on that night I never knew. He did not come to his usual bed in our room. Perhaps he was thrust into some 'black hole' to add to his sufferings. I never saw him again, for in a few days came the joyful news that my father had a situation."

Charles was ten years old when he left Chell workhouse. He had left school when he was seven, he had already had three different jobs. But now the blackest part of his life lay behind him. He described the exultant joy of that release from the bastille. Everything seemed sunshine and gladness. They came down the hill from Chell to Tunstall, on the high road this time, for they were no longer ashamed to face the world. Everybody welcomed them and was glad to see them again. They were free from the imprisoning walls, and at long last his father had work again. Their home was unfurnished, their supper was scanty, but they ate it all together, united after five weeks' separation. Their joy shone on their faces; they were free in their own home, life was beginning again.

Bob

THE SHIPWRECKED SHOEBLACK

TIMES were harsh, work was scarce in England in the 1840's. In Ireland the potato crop failed in 1845 and there was famine. Plenty of people starved to death in their homes, but 2,740,000 others between the years 1846–55 (according to government estimates of the time) tried to find a better life overseas. More prosperous families grew restless too. Mary Howitt's sister Emma and her husband had left for America in 1842; William and two of his sons went off in 1851 to look at Australia to see whether they wanted to make a home there for the family. Their journey would have been more comfortable, they would have chosen quicker ships than the passengers who travelled steerage in the emigrant vessels were able to afford.

The great majority of the people who left Great Britain and Ireland in those years went to North America. It was a golden land of promise where there was work and food. When you read the letters that they wrote home to announce their safe arrival you find continual, wondering mention of food – three meals a day, plenty of meat; an entirely new experience to people who had been hungry since their earliest infancy. For the hope of this they paid £3.10s. (£3.50p) or so to be carried over the North Atlantic by shipowners who, eager to make profits out of this new form of cargo, crammed as many human beings as they could in small, sometimes unseaworthy ships, manned by crews who were too often the scourings of the port.

The passengers travelled four to a berth, two or three tiers high. Plenty of people likened the conditions to those of a slave ship or an overcrowded jail. In times of storm they were battened down without light or air, and from the first day out their quarters stank like a cess-pool. Sea-sickness was one of the least of their worries, though they all suffered agonies from that, and those in the lowest tiers were obviously the worst placed. They had the prospect of seven to eight weeks at sea, a brutal and indifferent ship's crew, scanty food, little water, disease, perhaps death. Or their ship might be wrecked, like the *Annie Jane* in which a boy called R. C. Walters travelled in 1853.

He was a member of a London Ragged School. The Ragged Schools were a charitable body who gave destitute children teaching in the evenings, in the days before daytime schools were provided for everybody. They gave them other help too; some of them were supplied with brushes and polish so that they could set up as shoe-blacks and earn a little money. Some were helped to emigrate to the British Colonies. Australia was a favourite place at first, in spite of the terrifyingly long journey. But when the Gold Rush started in the '50's the Ragged School authorities had qualms about exposing their boys to the bad characters and the temptations that might be expected at the diggings, and they dispatched them only to Canada, where they might be expected to settle down quietly on farms.

And so on Tuesday, 23 August, 1853, they saw off eleven London boys from Liverpool. Among them was R. C. Walters who wrote out his experiences in a way that does credit to Ragged School teaching. It was printed in the Ragged School Magazine, who assured its readers that he had been given no help with it. They had not originally meant to use the account, but thought that it would be "a good lesson for him in composition and orthography" while he was recovering from his ordeal. He writes in a very formal way, to please his schoolteachers rather than his friends, and he never reveals his Christian name – it would have seemed far too

familiar. His friend appears just as an initial too. The grave gentlemen who ran the Ragged School expected decent restraint. But his name well might have been Robert, Bob for short.

The eleven boys had been taken up to Liverpool by "a gentleman from London who kindly officiated for us". He had shown them the sights of the city and they were all in high spirits when they embarked. But their troubles started almost at once. They had left Liverpool on 24 August. On the second day out they ran into a storm which carried away at one swoop the fore, main, and mizzen-topmasts, spars and rigging. "Nor were these our only misfortunes: besides the misery of a storm we had to suffer hunger – the boatswain refused to serve out the provision, and on the other hand it would have been impossible to have cooked anything, if we had it. As night came on, the rolling increased fearfully, and we were all in darkness. Chests flying about, children screaming, seamen cursing – in short it was such a scene as must be seen to be believed." Most of the crew were French Canadians, and could not understand the orders they were being given. The passengers, thoroughly unnerved, sent up a petition to the captain and persuaded him to turn back to Liverpool.

The *Annie Jane* reached Liverpool again on 2 September. The passengers made bitter complaints about the way they had been treated; a lot of them forfeited their fares rather than face the ship a second time. Three of the Ragged Boys retreated, and substitutes were sent for from London.

A week later, on 9 September, the ship, now repaired, set out again. Two days later, as before, a gale struck. The *Annie Jane*, laden with a cargo of railway iron, pitched and rolled horribly. And again the masts were swept away by the heavy seas. Below deck, Walters and another boy were sitting in their berth talking about – not home, for they probably had none, but "those we had left behind". At his friend's request, Walters read aloud a letter from the secretary from their old school. "He cried very much, and putting the note away, he said, 'Ah! I shall never see Mr W— again.' I tried to comfort him as much as I could, but I am afraid I proved a sorry comforter, being much in need of consolation myself."

Up on deck, the captain had first decided to turn for England a second time, but then had changed his mind; he was going to make for Canada whatever happened. When the angry passengers objected he called for his revolver and said he would shoot the first man that interfered between him and his duty. The danger increased, and the passengers were called on deck in the middle of the night and ordered to man the pumps. Three minutes at a time was all they could stand in those fearful seas, and meanwhile the crew tried to clear the broken spars and replace the foretop-mast.

Day and night the pumps were kept going, and the gale never slackened. They had been at sea for more than two weeks now. For the second time the foretop-mast was washed away, and the lifeboat followed it. The captain was defeated; the ship's head was turned for England and the nearest port. Walters, suffering agonies from sea-sickness, was below during most of this, but one of the other lads rushed down to him on the morning of 28 September to tell him there was great danger, they were running on to a reef of rocks. Walters would not listen at first, but another boy came down and said "He had seen some of the sailors shake hands."

He struggled into his clothes and found the deck crowded with panic-stricken passengers, screaming with fear, and more of them trying to get out. A seaman tried to quieten them by saying that there was no danger, they would be able to get off in boats in day-light. But he had hardly said so when Walters noticed another sea-man telling the cook that it was all up.

A moment or two later the ship struck the sands and Walters was

BETWEEN DECKS IN AN EMIGRATION VESSEL

thrown over and nearly smothered by the people who fell on top of him. He picked himself up, but was thrown again, and while he clung to an iron stanchion for support, there were passengers clinging to him. A distraught mother asked if he had seen her children. He had not. She rushed away and hurled herself down the hatchway.

The ship had now become a complete wreck, the greater part of the fore-cabin was broken up, and the passengers in this part of the ship were fighting to get through to the after-cabin, which they managed to do when a seaman smashed the partition with his hatchet. Here they found the captain, who was besieged on all sides by passengers desperate to know what hope of survival they had. He could only say " 'Let me go upon deck and attend to my duty.' " "G— went up to him, and shook hands with him; then turning to me, said, 'Walters, shake hands with the captain, and thank him for what he has done for us.' I obeyed mechanically; the captain said, 'God bless you, my dear boys.' "

Soon after this the water came in. Weak from his illness he tried to scramble towards the skylight overhead, but was pulled back by somebody below. Then a cask floated him up, and he found himself sitting on a table with a handful of passengers and the captain. And there he sat all night with nothing on but a blue checked shirt, and the water washing over him.

"The captain was standing just before me, with his head out of the broken skylight. I learned that the vessel had broke into three pieces, and we were floating about on the after-part of the wreck. I heard poor G— calling out to me for about twenty minutes; I answered him, and told him which way to come, but it seems he was jammed with the broken timbers, and the water rising gradually to his mouth gave the poor fellow a lingering death. It must have been about eleven o'clock when the vessel first struck, and it was not until about half-past six the next morning that we got off the wreck. The place where we were was strewn with broken fragments of the wreck, which kept floating about inside the cabin, maiming a great many of us. The deck above our heads was bending like a sheet of paper, and threatening to fall and crush us every instant.''

In the daylight he could see the chaos and destruction around him. Inside were naked men and women, half-dead with cold and fright; there were bodies buried under timbers. And when he scrambled out through the broken skylight it was worse. The ship had broken into three pieces. His part, the after-part, had been washed on to the shore, and being held fast by the shrouds, formed a bridge between the wreck and the shallow water.

There were rescuers standing on the shore—it was the small island of Barra in the Hebrides – and they brought a cart down to the water's edge. The women struggled along the mast and climbed into the cart; others waded ashore. But Barra was a poor community.

The survivors were taken to the only farm on the island, but not much comfort was to be had there.

"I repaired to a stable, and the farm servants having lit some fire, and there being an abundance of clean straw, we made ourselves as comfortable as our circumstances and situation would permit. Here I rather incautiously put my feet close to the fire, so that when I went to put my foot to the ground it caused me the greatest pain. While staying in these quarters we had to make a rather close acquaintance with some of the inhabitants of these regions; such as pigs and ducks, and small geese."

Walters said that there were 102 survivors – 8 cabin passengers, 61 steerage and 33 crew – which by his reckoning meant that 350 had died, among them nine of his Ragged School friends. They dug pits to bury the dead, but Walters, whose foot had been badly injured, was lying ill all this time.

The same ill fortune harried them when they tried to leave Barra a fortnight later. Boats were hired to take them to the mainland. But strong winds drove Walters and his companions off course, they were two days at sea, and eventually landed on Skye without any canvas. They plodded across the island by foot, wet and exhausted, to reach Portree. Here the inhabitants were sympathetic, and a subscription was got up in the kirk, and they lived in the local hotel until they could be sent to Glasgow by steam-packet.

At Glasgow Walters spent a week in the infirmary recovering from his injured foot, and then as soon as he could set off for Liverpool to ask the *Annie Jane*'s owners about his friend who had been saved with him from the wreck. But

"the owners told me they had neither seen nor heard anything of him, nor have we gleaned any tidings of the poor fellow yet. The owners gave me the money to defray my expenses, and I started the following day for London, where I am now staying, at the school in Bloomsbury. Since my return I have been enabled, by a few kind friends, to procure a passage to Australia, and, like Robinson Crusoe, am about to set out again in the wide world to try my fortune, trusting that by the goodness of God, and my own exertions, I may yet live to bless the day I first entered a Ragged School."

It was too early, when this article was printed, for the Ragged School Committee to know whether Walters had safely arrived. They could only say that he had sailed a few weeks before for Melbourne where he had a sister, who, they said would be "well able to sympathise with such a brother, as in going out she also was wrecked, and escaped only with her life." And the editor hoped "that the awful scenes witnessed by this youth have made a deep and salutary impression upon his mind, which, with God's blessing may result in a change of heart and life."

Willie, Florence and Nanny

SETTLERS IN OHIO

IN 1842 Mary Howitt's youngest sister Emma Alderson sailed for
America with her husband and three children. To Mary it was
deeply saddening; to her mother it must have seemed as though the
whole family was wrenched apart. The secluded life in the midlands
where it was an adventure to walk to the next valley was now a
thing of the past; her children were scattering further than she had
ever dreamed. Charles, the only boy in the family, had run away to
sea in 1825, and had died a few months later in Quebec, aged
seventeen. Mary was living in Germany (though she was to return),
and now Emma had gone. Harrison Alderson had taken the step
not only because he thought there would be better opportunities
for his children in America, but that there he could live a simpler
life more suited to his Quaker ideals.

Mary wrote from Germany to try to comfort her sister Anna: "Do
not, dear Anna, have doubts about Emma and her children; America
is the land for them – though I am sure that if they go with any
Utopian ideas of finding human nature better than in England they

will be disappointed." She added: "English papers contain the most doleful accounts of England – of course you know all – people starving and Sir Robert Peel laying on an Income Tax to cure all."

They never saw Emma again; she died five years later. They had been happy and prosperous years, and the two families had kept in close touch. Long letters crossed the Atlantic, lovingly chosen presents. The Howitts were eager for all news, not just of the Aldersons, but of American politics and the American way of life. America had been one of William's burning enthusiasms when he was a boy. He had read Winterbottom's *History of the United States*: "It had fired us up to a spirit of emigration, that, had we been as free to act as we were willing, would have carried us over to America, and turned us all into Republicans of the thoroughest grit. We were clamorous that our father should sell his property, take us over, and buy a 'wide, wide world' of his own – Howitt County at least."

Mary's mother remembered how her father had supported the grievances of the colonists during the War of Independence; Washington had been a hero to her; her father had spoken to her passionately too of the horror of slavery, how it demoralized the owner even more than the slave. The detestation of slavery that he aroused stayed with her all her life, and we have a glimpse of her in old age knitting objects to sell for the cause. Mary and William in the 1840's were taking part in anti-slavery conventions with other Quaker friends, and Emma in her letters wrote at length to them on the subject that she had as much at heart as they.

The Aldersons settled near Cincinnati, where Harrison farmed prosperously and wrote home with sober pleasure that the Quaker Meeting was at one with him over religious matters. The children grew and thrived; William Charles, Florence, and Nanny, and a baby daughter, Cornelia, or Nelly, born since the family had left England. In the year before she died, Emma kept a diary of her children's doings, so that Mary might make a book of it as she had made a book of her own children's daily lives. It appeared in 1849, with a sorrowing preface recalling that the Christmas recorded in it was Emma's last Christmas on earth.

It is very interesting to compare *The Children's Year* with *Our Cousins in Ohio* – Mary's book about her own children, with the one that she wrote about their American cousins. Anybody who has read American and English 19th century children's books side by side feels the difference; the American child emerges as sturdier, more independent, more self-reliant, while the Victorian English parents seem more concerned to keep their children young, and to shelter them from the outside world. And so it is with Herbert and Meggy Howitt and the little Aldersons in Ohio. The Howitt children play at being grown-up, with their toy cooking stove and their Swiss Family Robinson house. But from the very start Willy, Florence and even six-year-old Nanny take on this new American aspect; they have to do their share of duties in a household where there is no place for a separate child world.

It was a large and comfortable house, of which Emma had given enough details for Mary to be able to describe it at length.

"Their home was called 'The Cedars'; it was in the State of Ohio, on the banks of that noble river which gives its name to the State, and about four miles from the fine city of [Cincinnati]. 'The Cedars' lay upon a road which went on and on, through little clusters of houses and log cabins called 'towns' and 'villes' . . . It was a large, handsome, and somewhat commanding-looking place, a brick house, whitewashed, and one of the oldest thereabout.

"[It] had green Venetian outside shutters to the windows. In front there was a large two-storied porch, up which grew in wild luxuriance a beautiful prairie rose, which in summer hung about it like garlands of flowers. On the sunny side of the house, which was consequently very hot in summer, there ran along its whole length

AN EARLY SETTLER'S HOUSE IN TENNESSEE

a broad piazza; which, like the porch, was two-storied; so that both the upper and lower rooms opened into it. This piazza in winter was the favourite play-place of the children; and as it was shaded with vines and trumpet creepers, it was in warm weather like a beautiful summer parlour. Here, in summer, the family frequently took their meals, and often, after supper, sate in the delicious moonlight evenings, till bedtime."

The house stood in its own large grounds, approached from the road by an avenue of locust-trees, and its gardens were laid out with flowerbeds and shrubs, and shaded by the cedars and catalpas which had been part of the forest before the settlers had moved in to Ohio. Beyond the kitchen garden, the orchard and the vineyard, and the meadows that lay on their further side was

"an unbroken portion of the primeval forest, left uncleared purposely for a supply of firewood; and from this cause its beautiful timber was fast vanishing away. From time to time a noble hickory or sugar-maple was felled and cut up; and this our friends never failed to deplore, for they yet retained the Englishman's love of trees; and they were here continually reminded of what is a very common experience in America: 'Never,' say the lovers of the picturesque there, 'set your heart upon a tree; for as sure as you do, somebody will come with an axe and cut it down.'"

143

This wood where the children and their mother picked flowers in spring and summer, and went nutting in the autumn, was known as Jack's wood, and belonged to a blind negro doctor, Doctor Jack. Emma had much to say about Doctor Jack. He had been a slave in the South for the greater part of his life, and his children had all been taken from him and sold to various masters. About twenty-five years before the Aldersons had come, he had scraped together 250 dollars to buy his own freedom, and 350 for his wife, she being much younger. He practised as a doctor in Cincinnati, and saved enough money to buy the farm on which Jack's Wood stood.

"These people, however, were much to be pitied, because, as they were black, they could get nobody to do anything for them, and now that the old man was unable to cultivate his land himself, it lay waste, and it was to be feared that the time when they would know want, was not far distant. The lower class who lived in the neighbourhood were mostly German settlers, and they had, it was very difficult to say why, almost a stronger prejudice against people of colour than the Americans themselves, and they were treated by them with great indignity and unkindness. For instance, the Germans had, during the preceding winter, fitted up an old barn as a theatre, which was all very well in itself and as a means of their own innocent amusement; but, unfortunately, it was made the means of exciting ridicule and persecution against the poor oppressed blacks; for here they were made the especial objects of vulgar derision and abuse."

At the time that Emma was keeping her diary, Doctor Jack was gradually failing through old age, and the Aldersons did what they

could to help him and his wife. On Good Friday of that year the
children took him a pie, and a few days later some apples, and
bravely walked up to the house with them, though they were all
frightened of the savage dogs that Doctor Jack kept to ward off
intruders. Their father, when he heard that the old man's wife could
not take her butter and eggs to market because she was not able to
leave her husband, sent down to buy them himself. But the next
time they went to ask after Doctor Jack, his wife sorrowfully said –
"Oh! Sir, he's gone home – gone! Paid the debt that we must all
sooner or later pay!" He had been buried in his own wood, and a
month later Mr Hudson, the coloured preacher, would come and
"preach a funeral". However, the story seemed to end happily. On
Sunday, 28 May, 1846 they called on Mrs Jack to see how she was
going on.

"As usual, the dogs barked outrageously, and she popped out of
the porch. She was very grand in a new black dress, although her
customary coloured handkerchief was bound on her head. Every-

body thought her quite magnificent. The sailor-farmer, her new bailiff, was sitting in the house with her: he was reading the Bible; and being now seen by our friends for the first time, was discovered to be a handsome coloured man, not yet middle-aged, very well-dressed and intelligent-looking. The old lady seemed remarkably cheerful, and told them with great glee that the man's wife and children were going to live with her, and that she expected to be very comfortable, and to make a good living this year.

"The children's father inquired of 'the funeral' and when it was to be preached, as they wished to hear Mr Hudson, the black preacher. As soon as this was spoken, there was a perfect scream from the old woman. 'The funeral' had been preached that very morning, and she or her man Jerry, they could not rightly understand which, had forgotten to sent them word; and now she did not know how to make apologies enough; however, they should know next time, that she was determined, even if 'the funeral' was preached for herself. She informed them, however, that 'a right smart company was there,' and that it was, she could assure them, a very good funeral!"

The Aldersons were deeply troubled about the slavery problem. It was a cause that the Quakers traditionally championed, and in any case one of the aspects of American life that the educated immigrant most disliked. The American visitor to England commented with horror on the swarms of beggars and the degradation of the working classes, their English counterparts in America on the effects of slavery. Mary Howitt, as preoccupied as Emma with this issue, tells in the book how the children's Uncle Cornelius had seen the arrival in Ohio of 395 emancipated slaves. They had been the property of a wealthy North Carolina planter who in his lifetime had been one of the most strenuous and violent upholders of slavery, but in his will had provided not only for the liberation of all his slaves after his death, but for their transport to a state where they might be free and for their maintenance there.

This story had a sad ending. When they arrived at the end of the journey, a brutal mob refused to allow them into the land that had been bought for them in Mercer County, Ohio.

"Amid all these vicissitudes of weather, drenching rain, extreme cold, and then again burning heat, these poor, unfortunate emigrant negroes from Roanoke were encamped in the woods bordering the canal, and unable to enter upon their new homes; because those homes and lands and provisions, for which they had paid 30,000 dollars, were forbidden to them by the neighbouring settlers, who were resolutely determined not to have them amongst them. . . . They had indeed no place of refuge. They were forbidden to set foot in the land which their own money had purchased; nor as free negroes could they return to their former homes in a Slave State."

There had been at The Cedars a coloured woman servant who had been born into slavery, and had told them of her sufferings. Her father was a wealthy white planter in Georgia; she had been sold when she was six, and treated as a favourite until she had one day fallen asleep while brushing her mistress's hair, whereupon she had been so severely flogged that it nearly killed her. When the family moved to Indiana where they could not keep her as a slave, they offered her her freedom for four hundred dollars, which by incessant washing and nursing she managed to lay by. But by this time she had a small son, and he was a slave still, and her mistress used to threaten that she would send the boy back to Georgia. In despair she ran away with the boy disguised as a girl. They eluded their pursuers, and were lucky enough to find shelter in a tavern whose owner was an abolitionist and hid them for several weeks. The boy Paul was a clever lad and the inn-keeper contrived to get him apprenticed to a shoemaker.

All this had happened some years before. Adele, the mother, had left the Aldersons to marry a free coloured man in Cincinnati, and Paul was doing well at his trade. Then, on 27 September, 1846, Emma records:

"Early in the day, two handsome, well-grown coloured lads made their appearance at The Cedars; and to the surprise of every one, the taller was recognized as Paul, Adele's boy, as he was called. They might well hardly know him, he was so much grown, and so well-dressed. He was come, he said, merely to make a call on them before leaving the city, where he had been to see his mother in her new home; and his companion was Joe, a friend of his.

"Paul was dressed in a suit of blue. He said he had come from Columbia to see his mother, and that now he had seen her so comfortable, he should go back with a light heart.

"After Paul had told this, and exhausted all his polite speeches, he asked if he might take a look round the place, for he had been telling Joe, he said, as they came along, all about it, and of the adventures which he and Willie used to have together. Joe was a stout-built coloured lad, very demure apparently, and apparently also very much on his good behaviour, although a great deal of fun was visible in his jet-black eyes, and at the corners of his wide mouth.

"Willie, who was thoroughly English in his feelings on many subjects, had no American prejudices on the score of colour, and therefore he set off very well pleased to accompany the two black visitors.

"In the course of their ramble, they went to Jack's wood, where they found so many hickory-nuts on the trees, that Paul climbed into some and shook them down by showers. They then collected them, and found that there were upwards of a bushel and a half, with which they were well pleased.

"They returned home to dinner as hungry as hunters, and greatly enjoyed the pot-pies made of boiled chicken, potatoes and pastry, which were set smoking hot on the table as they entered, and the huge slices of pumpkin-pie which came afterwards. Poor Paul was wonderfully well-behaved; he attended to all the little customary proprieties, which were always regarded at table at The Cedars, and said, 'Thank you,' and 'Yes, sir, if you please,' or 'No, I thank you, ma'am,' when invited to take more, and ate with great quietness and decorum. Willie heard him instructing Joe in good manners while they were out; and in whispers, and by elbow-jogs he reminded him of the same during dinner; and in excuse for some breach of good manners in Joe, which he thought must not be allowed to pass unobserved, he said. 'You must excuse Joe, he ain't used to eat at white people's tables.'

"When they left, Willie and Nanny accompanied them to the gate, and were filled with indignation and grief, to see that no sooner were they on the road than a carter, passing in his cart, shouted out to them, 'Well, Nigger, where do you come from?' and a boy, a little farther on, threw clods of dirt at them, and shouted, 'Nigger!' "

Nearly every English visitor remarked how Americans seemed to notice no difference in rank or class, but addressed one as an equal. Some deplored this, a few admired it, but all were astonished. The Aldersons accepted it; in their household the servants sat down to meals with the family, "according to the universal custom in this country", and we have seen how coloured visitors shared their meals – which was not the universal custom.

But when it came to the difficulty of finding white servants, Emma Alderson wrung her hands and lamented as every prosperous European settler had done before her. She tried to find a woman who would help with the washing, but no one would come. She asked a poorly-clad boy if he thought his mother would be willing.

" '*My* mother!' returned the boy, who seemed astonished, 'she can't go; and if she could she wouldn't.'

"After this unsuccessful attempt, which was characteristic enough of common American life, they went first to one and then to another, offering handsome wages if some good woman would please to come and wash; but some women were too busy, and some offended at being asked such a thing.

"At length they met with one woman poor enough to work for another; but even she consented to do it as a great favour, and with a request that it should be kept secret from her husband. Singularly enough this woman, although no one could doubt but that the sixty cents a day which would be paid her, were very acceptable, exhausted all her stock of reasoning and eloquence to prove to the children's mother that there really was no degradation in going out to work and to wash for other people, and for a neighbour especially. 'To be sure there was not!' the mother said over and over again. The poor woman came and did the washing; yet still a lingering dissatisfaction with herself seemed to rest on her own mind.

"The mother said with a sigh, as she had often before done on such occasions, how different things were in Old England, where there were only too many washerwomen for the linen . . . Another sigh the good mother heaved, for she saw in this reluctance to do daily labour the hateful effects of slavery, which had made labour and degradation synonymous words."

Ample employment meant there were no beggars – an astonishing thing for eyes who were used to thousands of beggars in every English city. Meggy and Herbert Howitt, the English cousins in *The Children's Year*, certainly knew all about them, sheltered though their lives were. The toy cooking stove which gave them so much pleasure had been bought from a shivering, half-starved boy in the street, who hawked them for his father. There was nothing like this in America.

"It was a very rare thing for a beggar to be seen by our cousins. Perhaps once a month or so one might present himself; and in consequence, a beggar was an object of great compassion, and was treated with much kindness, often receiving silver as an alms, and always being invited to rest, and to partake of the next meal, let it be what it would."

But there had been one incident which was very reminiscent of England where begging had become a trade and a way of life. Two very poor, wretched and ragged men had called at The Cedars one Sunday. They said they were emigrants from the south of Ireland, had come to New Orleans and had suffered a great deal by fever and the death of friends. "Everybody compassionated these 'poor Irish', and everything, therefore, was done for them that could be, and which the children thought was not half enough."

But when the family set off for Meeting an hour later, they passed the beggars whom they had supplied an hour before with food and money. They were dressed as beggars no longer; the blind one had recovered his sight, and they were busy stowing away their tatters.

ATTACK ON A POTATO STORE IN IRELAND

It was particularly mortifying that they were Irishmen, for there was immense sympathy for the Irish at that time. 1845 was the year of the potato failure in Ireland, by 1846 there was famine.

"Nanny, who heard so much of this 'horrible famine' in Ireland, which destroyed thousands of men, women, and children, pictured to herself a huge monster, like an ancient dragon, which swallowed up whole provinces at a mouthful. At length, however, she, as well as the rest, were made perfectly to understand what this new and strange misery meant, and then their sympathy for the poor starving people was unspeakable. If they sate down to a remarkably good and plentiful dinner, they wished that the children of poor Ireland could do the same. If any of them were dissatisfied with what was set before them, the others would gravely lecture on the sinfulness of ingratitude when such thousands were wanting bread.

"After the great talk of the famine, came the great talk of what America should do to relieve the sufferings of their distant kinspeople in Ireland; and subscription on subscription was set on foot to purchase provisions and other things for their relief."

The Alderson children did what they could. Willy sold one of his guinea-hens, and made shoe-pegs for the wooden-soled shoes worn by the country people. He made his hands very sore, but he whittled away hundreds which were bought by the local shoemaker. Florence undertook needlework for her mother, and sewed two pillow-cases. So that when Willy went with his parents to Cincinnati on 22 November

"he carried with him a dollar, the joint earnings of himself and his sisters, together with his favourite English shilling, which was paid in towards the subscription for the suffering Irish. His mother also took with her warm, quilted bedcovers, and petticoats, and many comfortable garments, which she had had made for these poor people."

English children would have been encouraged to make just the same sort of efforts to help the less fortunate, but what would not have been usual in England was the part that Willy, Florence and Nanny were expected to take in the duties of the household. On 29 July his mother wrote:

"An active boy of nine can do a great deal if he only sincerely wishes to make himself useful.

"He was up at five o'clock in the morning, and before breakfast went some distance to desire the seamstress to come to work. He

next went to Athens for groceries; came back, said his lessons, and went into the garden to collect the weeds which his father had pulled up in the early morning, he then dug up potatoes for dinner. After dinner, he went with his sisters to gather blackberries, and brought home five quarts. He then helped little Frederick Lotte to carry boards for flooring the new portico, and with Nanny's help cleared away a deal of rubbish. After this he made a nice little house out of an old box, for the puppies. Nanny provided the hay for the bed, the softest she could find; and thus all were left very comfortable. He then had his supper, watched the men at work at the portico, fetched up the cows, gave them their salt, blacked his own shoes, and brushed his clothes, the next day being Sunday, and went to bed very happy, because every body was well satisfied with him."

The English cousins would certainly have had to do their lessons before they were allowed to play, but at The Cedars there were not only lessons, but work for everybody. On 25 October the children were in tears when they thought of all they had to do before they

could go to Jack's Wood to collect the nuts. There were the lessons, then Willy had to husk corn, and with six-year-old Nanny's help he picked the green tomatoes to feed to the pigs. Meanwhile Florence, who was eight, was looking after Nelly, the two-year-old baby – until she remembered that the shoes she needed for the afternoon's expedition were still with the shoemaker, so she had to leave Nelly to Nanny's care, and walk off to fetch them. There was time for the nutting, but they were so sleepy by the evening that they fell asleep while their father was reading to them.

There were all sorts of seasonal activities too, in which the whole family took part, like picking raspberries, and paring and slicing peaches for "peach leather" (dried pulp). In the winter evenings they settled down to make a rag-carpet.

"In England nobody understands what rag-carpets are; but in every part of America they are more or less used. The wealthy use them for their kitchens and sometimes dining rooms; the farmers, for their chambers; and often every room in the house will be covered with them. . . . [The family at The Cedars] were making a rag-carpet for their common sitting-room; and the manner of its making was this: –

"Every conceivable kind of woollen cloth was cut into little shreds about half an inch wide, and an inch long. These were all joined together lengthwise, and then wound in balls. The children's employment was to help in sewing the shreds together, and thus to make hundreds and thousands of yards of woollen band. This was afterwards woven into a coarse kind of carpet, and produced a mottle of all colours, not at all unpleasing to the eye. Occasionally such carpets would be dyed all of one colour; sometimes they were woven into a regular pattern, stripe or plaid; but this which was making at the Cedars, was to be a mottled one; and their young friends the Munroes, Henry, Eugene and Ada, were invited for a few days to help in this homely but curious work; during which, however, some amusing book was read, and thus the time passed pleasantly."

There is, however, plenty of detail about the games that the children played between their tasks. Emma described the ones that would be strange to English readers. There was hog-driving, for instance, when they played at driving a herd of three thousand hogs to California. Willy, the drover, met all sorts of hazards on the way; some of the hogs strayed in the woods, others were attacked by wolves, before he got them safe over the Rocky Mountains and delivered to Nanny, the settler in California. Sometimes they played at taking rafts of timber down the Ohio, or at slave drivers. There was sledging too, and making pop-corn on a hot fire-shovel. The diary is full of the delights of the passing seasons – the moment that it could be said that spring was come, and they could sit on the piazza in the evening singing hymns; the lovely May morning when the table was laid for breakfast on the piazza, "and a cry of delight escaped the children as they came down at the sight."

Emma might sometimes long for the sound of the English lark, but in autumn she daily wished she could show her English friends how glorious the American Fall was. She described in several entries in the diary the splendour of the orchards under an intensely blue sky and brilliant white clouds, the garden rich with flowers, and the piazza now overhung with dark clusters of purple grapes. After four years in America, she still found the colouring of the forest trees awe-inspiring.

"There still remained almost every variety of green, intermingled with every shade of yellow, orange, red, brown, and occasionally deep purple. Here and there, the trunks and arms of gigantic dead trees would be wreathed with Virginian creepers of the most intense scarlet, often starting forth from the very thickest of the forest, like a fantastic scarlet tower."

One October day the children and their friends, Henrietta and Frank, newly arrived from England, went on a fishing excursion to a wild and solitary valley called Bald-face Creek. Willie carried his new fishing-rod which he paid for with half a bushel of newly-gathered nuts. Florence, Frank, and Willie fished, and the others searched for fossil shells and corals in the rocky stream. Then they spread their lunch of cheese-cake, pasties and sandwiches on a smooth table of slaty rock, and twisted up button-wood leaves to make drinking cups. The sedate English Henrietta at first tried to keep the company in order, and then gave it up. "Then what shouts and laughter echoed through the wood, each one trying to do something crazier than the other." They picked ripe paw-paws in the woods, decked themselves in leaves, waded in the stream (even Henrietta), and arrived home "wreathed like a party of young Bacchanals".

It was an idyllic day, one of those of pure happiness which are only possible in childhood, when you can live in the present, and the happiness is undiluted by thoughts of past or future. The Christmas of that year was the same; the last Christmas that the children would spend with their mother. There had not been much money for them to spend on their presents as they had given all their savings to the starving Irish. The little girls had stitched away to make theirs, and Willie with the money he had left, had bought for Florence a figure of Queen Victoria nursing the Prince of Wales, a clockwork windmill for Nanny, and a trumpet for Nelly, while for his mother he had

borrowed money from his father to buy a plaster of Paris dove. He had gone to Cincinnati to do his shopping, and had wandered round the market afterwards. It was full of food for Christmas – venison, opossums, squirrels, wild turkey, and four bears which had been fattened and killed by the butchers. "They looked very strange, having their huge black paws, and black muzzles still left on; otherwise the flesh did not look unlike veal."

The Christmas celebrations started on Christmas Eve, with the sound of people firing off guns and pistols. Uncle Cornelius and their cousin Michael came and fired at the door of The Cedars, to their great joy. Then, Christmas Day!

"Willie was up by five o'clock, and Florence and Nanny were not long after him. The shoes on the hearth, the best shoes for the day's visiting, were found filled with presents. Queen Victoria and the Prince, and the wonderful windmill, and the trumpet, were there, and so many other things that the shoes would not hold them. Besides the brimful shoes, the little table near the hearth was covered with presents, of which nobody had any idea – none of the little folks at least. There were new dresses for them all – new silk-aprons for the little girls, even for Nelly – new winter-bonnets – new fur-tippets and muffs, and all sorts of things. . . .

"Among the other shoes stood also the best shoes of the beloved mother. That really was a surprise to her; and in one of them sate Willie's snow-white dove! How happy it made him to see that she was greatly pleased. She put it on the chimney piece of her own room; and it was the prettiest ornament there."

The children were invited to spend the day with friends in Cincinnati, and all dressed in their new Christmas clothes they set off at nine o'clock with the German farmer who farmed their father's land, and a crowd of German settlers, all in a huge covered wagon. There was no prohibition about celebrating Christmas as there had been in their mother's childhood, and they spent a supremely happy day with their friends and a great company of guests.

"The furniture had all been removed from one large room; and here they played at all imaginable games – blind-man's-buff, turn the trencher, forfeits and the rest, – and then supper was announced, and each little boy, taking a little girl by the hand, led her to the supper-table. And what a supper there was! There was tea and cakes, and fruit and sweetmeats, and pies of every possible kind, and cheese-cakes and candies, and heaped-up plates of sugar-kisses wrapped in bright coloured paper with mottoes; and huge cakes covered with sugar; and there they sate eating and talking, and laughing, and the grown-up people waiting on them, and laughing, and as merry as anybody.

"As soon as supper was over, it was announced to our cousins that Eberhard was waiting at the door with the wagon, and afterwards he had to call for the women and the children, so Willie and his sisters took their leave, and having called for the German women, they all drove off amid the most glorious Christmas moonlight, the Germans singing beautiful hymns as they drove along. . . . O it was a wonderful day!"

FOR UNITED AMERICAN STATES,
A THRIVING REPUBLIC, WHOSE ORIGIN DATES
FROM SEVENTEEN HUNDRED AND EIGHTY-THREE
WHEN BRITAIN ACKNOWLEDGED AMERICA FREE,

Samuel

COACHES AND RAILWAYS

Writing in 1923, the year that he died, Samuel Cooper Scott – then a Canon of Chester – could remember events as far back as 1840.

"The first event I can remember was the marriage of Queen Victoria to Prince Albert, known afterwards as the Prince Consort. This took place on February 10th, 1840, so that I was not quite two years old. . . . What I remember is this. Looking out of our nursery window, we saw the ships dressed with flags from end to end; we saw the various trade processions pass with bands playing and with banners on two poles, stayed up against the wind with ropes and tassels, the Foresters with green scarves and bows; shepherdesses with crooks and ribbons. The maids ran out to see the fun, and my brother John and I seized on two sticks, to which we tied a woollen scarf, and paraded round the nursery with our banner."

Down in London middle-aged William Howitt, republican in his feelings though he was, could be stirred by the sight of the young Queen, radiant, driving to a banquet at the Guildhall. In Hull the Scott boys could not remember a time when there had not been a queen, and they were strongly royalist.

Their father was vicar of St Mary's, Lowgate, in Kingston-on-Hull, a city dominated by its docks. Soon after the birth of Samuel, the family moved to a house on the dockside, near the Monument Bridge in the Old Town, opposite the Old Dock near the end of Whitefriargate, and the nursery window looked down upon it. They were not a wealthy family, and Samuel was uneasily aware of the struggle his parents had to make ends meet – though his father used to forget the fact from time to time and go out on book-hunting expeditions, bringing back, to Mrs Scott's despair, yet more booty to add to his hoard. Samuel, watching his mother wearily mending the family's clothes as they came back from the wash, once asked if it wouldn't be easier for him to wear hob-nail boots and corduroy trousers like working boys. But she smiled, and said the nails would wear holes in the carpet.

The docks dominated Hull, and they were the Scott boys' chief interest. Most of the day they spent at the window watching the ships come through the bridge into the Old Dock. Steam ships were a novelty, most of what they saw below them were sailing vessels. There were whalers, which smelt dreadful. These were laid up in the docks in the winter, the whale boats stacked on the decks, the holds

full of casks for the oil. There was a day in the 1840's when he remembered a great commotion in the streets and crowds running. He ran with them, without the least idea where they were going, and was swept along to the pier. "There, about half a mile off, lay a whaler, the crow's nest (a cask high up on the mast from which a man looked out for the blowing of a whale) was in its place; the huge jawbones of a whale were set up against the foremast reaching nearly to the 'top'. . . The excitement was intense. The whaler had been nipped in the ice, and had been kept amongst the icefields throughout the winter, and no doubt there were fears that she was altogether lost."

Most of the ships in the Old Dock came from Baltic and North Sea ports. There were fast fruit schooners too; the orange clippers were particularly beautiful vessels with a fragrant smell. Their unloading was spectacular. The porters ran with practised ease up a succession of planks that bent under them to empty the crates of oranges balanced on their heads into the upper stories of the warehouses.

Even better was the unloading of the grain ships. The boys watched the baskets being filled in the holds and hauled up on ropes by men standing in the shrouds, and then emptied into a canvas spout which carried the grain into a lighter moored alongside the vessel.

Then there was the timber dock, where logs floated temptingly. Samuel and John used to run over them, the water squirting up between the dipping and swaying floor. But one horrifying day John fell between two logs and had to be dragged out by his hair. A relation saw the sodden, dripping boy being hurried home, and that particular game came to an end.

There were however other opportunities for delicious daring – for instance, jumping the bridges that connected the old and the new towns at the locks of the various docks. These were raised when ships went through; a bell rang and anybody who wanted to escape being held up ran to get over in time, and the boldest jumped the gap as the bridge moved up. A more sedate pleasure was watching the windmills. The city was full of them for the factories there used wind power rather than steam. They ringed the docks, and from their window the Scott boys could see the whirling sails, and wait for the men to come out on the galleries to attend to them. Their father sometimes took them on his visits to ships in the docks, and they were allowed to prowl around and look at the birds and animals that the sailors had brought back with them. The baby bears, in particular, were delightful to play with.

In the 1840's life was changing fast. Samuel Scott was a Victorian; but in his childhood there was plenty to remind him of an earlier age. There were the Quakers who still wore the clothes of a past generation, the women in soft greys with beautiful white bonnets, delicate stockings, and sandalled feet, the men in drab coats, white falling neckcloths and knee breeches. There were the elections, savage affairs, highly popular with the rowdier inhabitants, who might not have a vote but did have a chance of doing a little damage.

"The time of canvass was long and very exciting; blue rosettes were provided, and we wore them in our jackets and walked about the streets in them. Feeling ran high; a boy snatched my rosette from my jacket and threw it in the gutter. I pursued him and pummelled him.

"The hustings were erected in front of the Town Hall, great baulks of timber supporting a substantial platform capable of holding a very large number of people and of resisting any attacks that might be made on it. We were taken to a shop next to it; we could look on to the platform, which stretched out much in front of the shops, and if we could not hear the words of the speakers, we could see their emphatic gestures. The whole space in front of the hustings was filled with a shouting, jeering, howling mass of men and boys, with women here and there. The groaning and cheering went on the whole time. The proposers and seconders and candidates were inaudible. Every now and then a fight arose, blows were struck, and blood flowed; banners were raised up and torn down; symbols of poor feeding, the red herring, the small loaf, the large loaf, etc., were hoisted up on poles and were greeted with yells and counteryells. Eggs, oranges, refuse from the market were thrown. This wild, savage scene was thought to be as important a part of an election as the voting itself. Some ladies sat it out in the Town Hall windows and even on the hustings.

"The election was fought on the Free Trade and Protection tickets. The Corn Laws had but been recently abolished, and feeling ran very high indeed. The Liberal candidates were elected, a petition was filed, and they were unseated for bribery. The inquiry went on for a long time, and it was quite the thing for people of leisure to attend and enjoy the examination of their fellow-townsmen."

People with faces pitted like nutmeg-graters were a reminder of the menacing disease that smallpox had been in the previous century, before vaccination had become general. And there was cholera, the most terrifying of the epidemic diseases of the early 19th century. With improved water supplies and drainage, it was to die out in the second half of the century, but there was a bad outbreak in 1849, when everybody who could left Hull, and the Scott children were sent into the Lake District.

And from the 20th century, Canon Scott could look back at the coaching age. The improved surface of the roads at the beginning of the 19th century had made coach transport efficient for the first time. After thirteen hundred years or so the country had managed to struggle back to roads comparable to those the Romans had laid down. The mail coach had twenty or thirty years of glory, and then they had to give way to the railways. Canon Scott had been born in the railway epoch; every year they were spreading their tentacles further. But there were still coaches galloping between the towns when he was a boy, and the people who used them were cheerfully confident that the iron roads were a passing fancy that would not last.

By the time he was ten he could go to visit his uncle in Lincoln by rail, but before that he used to make the journey by coach, put in charge of the guard or a friendly passenger.

"In the summer I remember sitting on the top near the driver; we whirled along with four horses through villages, the people and children running out to see the coach and hear the guard's horn, which was freely used. We would stop, perhaps at a road-end, where a cart would be waiting with a box or a traveller, a girl going to service, possibly; they would be hoisted on to the coach, then with expressions of mutual goodwill we were off again, and the little cart, when its occupant had watched us out of sight, would turn back to its dull little life in some out-of-the-world hamlet, and things would go on as before, until, perhaps, the traveller would return to pay her friends a visit and bring a little town air and gossip with her. Sometimes it would be a dog cart, with a groom who waited for a parcel which the coach was to bring. The guard sat behind on a little seat, and seemed almost to hang on to the coach; he was always busy, tightening the luggage straps, wrapping a coat round some one, blowing his horn. At the top of the hill down he came to put

London. Pub by A. PARK. 47 Leonard St.

THE MAIL CHANGE.

on the shoe drag, at the bottom down again to take it off and hang it up under the coach. If any passenger had to get up or alight, the ladder was needed.

"Then there were the stopping places, where the horses were changed and the passengers got down to stretch their legs and get rid of the stiffness incidental to sitting on a coach, where you were sometimes cramped into torture. There were the letter bags to drag out of the locker, and the new ones to put in; there was the house of change with its hospitable bar, hoping for some one to do something 'for the good of the house'; then the start again, each time like a new journey, and the horses really liking it for a mile or so.

"Once I made a part of the journey in the dark, and spent the time inside the coach amongst a lot of straw and some most uninteresting people, who were close, if not good, company. We jolted against each other, slept, and were awakened by some one having lost consciousness and tumbling against his neighbour. Then we

165

reached the lighted streets of Lincoln, and blinked at them as they at us, turned in under the archway of the inn yard, and were picked out piece by piece as stiff as frozen rabbits; and then a cab, or what answered to one, took us and our luggage home.

"Another journey was made when there was snow on the ground. The sun shone brightly. I sat on the top and was covered up and kept warm by kindly passengers, who were very sociable in those days and really helped each other. Coach travellers were, for the time being, a family. When we stopped to change horses, and I was lifted off, I could scarcely tell when my feet reached the ground, except that I could go no further down."

(That visit to Lincoln was memorable because he saw a Christmas tree for the first time, at the house of some German friends. It was a huge tree reaching to the ceiling, glorious with candles and toys. But when he was asked to choose a present, he shyly pointed to the smallest he could see – a drum filled with sweets. In 1923 he was still regretting this choice.)

The railway had come to Hull some years before it ever reached Lincoln. Samuel was only two, but he remembered the excitement of the first train running out of Hull on 2 July, 1840. The children were taken to the top windows of one of the houses that overlooked the station (which was little more than a shed, with wooden plat-forms). There were flags and decorations and huge crowds, and when the train came in the engine was decked with flags and garlands, too.

"In the evenings the railway company ran trains a few miles out of Hull and back again just to show people what it was like and accustom them to the new-fangled way of travelling, which was by old people, and some younger also, viewed with the greatest suspicion and distaste; there were many people then who would never enter a train, and who died boasting they had never done so. The carriages on such occasions were mere cattle trucks, with planks across them for seats. . .

"The early models of railway carriages were peculiar. They were called coaches, and the first-class carriages were shaped like the bodies of three stage coaches set upon a platform with wheels, the second-class were more box-like, and very rudely furnished inside; while the descent from second to third class was one hardly to be

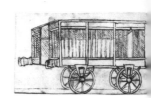

believed; the value of the third-class passenger as a dividend-paying person had not dawned upon the minds of railway proprietors. . . . The carriage appointed then for the use of a third-class passenger was a long square box, with sides breast-high and above that entirely open to the sky, so that he was soaked in wet weather, either directly from the clouds or indirectly from the umbrellas of his fellow-travellers, while in hot weather he was baked by the sun which blistered the seats of the carriages, was covered with black and smuts from the engine, and now and then had to stamp out a spark which sometimes burned a hole in the traveller's clothes before it reached the floor.

"There was one seat in the middle of the side of this conveyance; a seat of the knifeboard order ran down the centre, while other seats were at the sides and ends. A further discouragement shown to the third-classer was that he could only travel in this hideous discomfort by starting at about 6 a.m., and that by a train which stopped at every station. As late as 1852 I set off with my brother on a journey to Cheltenham in one of these affairs. We did not reach Derby until about 3 o'clock, and there we stayed the night with friends, the third-class train going no further that day.

"On the occasion of such a journey as this we used to be early at the station, make a rush for the train as soon as it backed to the platform, secure if possible the middle of the seat at the back end of the third-class carriage nearest the engine, which was partially sheltered by the higher carriage in front, for these open carriages were mercifully placed between the higher ones; then, with an umbrella over us to protect us from the wind and rain, a rug to cover our legs and feet, and a novel between us, we were fixed as far as human foresight could go for the day; one of us held the umbrella, and the other turned over the leaves of the book, and woe to the slower reader at the exciting parts of Dickens or Marryat. The carriages were not so well coupled as now, and the motion from side to side of the truck was not pleasant, while the sight of the higher carriage running behind emphasised the motion of the tub in which we were riding, and had a sea-sick effect about it.

"Second-class carriages had no cushions or padding of any kind, no luggage racks, no blinds, and, in later times, it was quite a piece of good luck to find one with a cold slippery covering of American cloth. They were unwarmed, and rugs, such as were used on the stage coaches, were needed. To carry out the stage coach idea, the guards in charge of the train wore red coats and sat on a seat on the top of the end carriage. From this seat, by turning a handle, they were able to put on a brake. This was soon changed when the speed of the trains was increased and there were tales told of guards whose heads had broken as the trains passed under bridges.

"A low railing surrounded the carriage top, and on the top the luggage was piled, covered with tarpaulins and strapped down to the rail; sometimes the strap, when it got loose, would flap about and dash against the window in a very alarming way. Boards, with hooks to catch on to the railing, were provided at the stations, and the luggage was slid down the incline."

The Great Exhibition is the obvious landmark that divides the lean hungry years of the early part of the century from the prosperity of the later half. It was not just a national wonder, it was an international one. The streets of London were thronged, as Mary Howitt told her sister in her letters, with dazed, bemused foreigners who had come to see this great sight. They were also thronged with people from the provinces who had never in their lives been in the capital city, who had perhaps never stirred more than a mile or two from their homes. It was the railways that had brought them there, at a price that they could afford. If the exhibition had been staged forty or fifty years earlier, in the Howitts' childhood, it would not

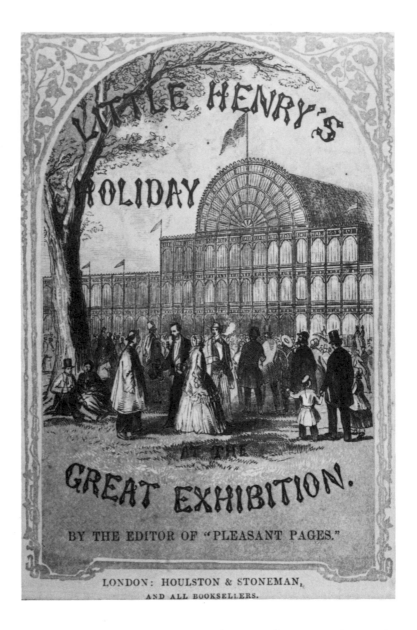

LITTLE HENRY'S HOLIDAY AT THE GREAT EXHIBITION.

BY THE EDITOR OF "PLEASANT PAGES."

LONDON: HOULSTON & STONEMAN, AND ALL BOOKSELLERS.

have been a national event; in the absence of transport it could only have interested the Londoners.

The Scott boys were among those who went down by railway to see the great sight. Their father, who had a keen sense of drama, led them into the vast glass palace with their eyes shut. They were not to open them until he said. He took them to the front of the gallery and then said they might look.

"The variety of colour, the bright sunshine, the throng of people, the sound of their voices, the distant music, the great crystal fountain in the centre throwing up abundance of water, with its grateful plashing sound and rainbow colouring, the trees, plants and creepers which hung from the gallery fronts, silenced us. It was all beyond words, and we stayed a long time looking on before we attempted to examine the wonders which were exhibited in the various courts. On shilling days the place was crowded with working people, who brought their children. In the transepts were the large elm trees, which gave a delightful shade, for the glaring light was rather trying at times; there were open courts round these trees, with fountains and gold fish in the basins; tables were set out for refreshments, and the people brought their own food and sat about, while the children sat on the marble borders of the tanks and splashed the water with their hands. There was a freedom about it all, a good humour, a sense of holiday, a novelty, which had something of enchantment."

THE SHILLING DAY RUSH TO THE EXHIBITION

Samuel was thirteen then. Three years later, in 1854, that first carefree part of his life finished for ever. He was sixteen, his father could afford to educate him no longer, and he went off to work as a clerk in a private bank in Derby. "I went to Derby on 4 July, 1854, and my no.2 life began from this time. I had a miserable toothache, and lay awake all night, but on the next day I entered upon my duties."

It amused him in 1923 to remember those duties and the building where he performed them – they belonged to an age which had been swept away.

"The bank building was a very old-fashioned place . . . The door was up a narrow passage. Further up the passage was the front door of the bank house, where the senior clerk lived, and beyond this were some buildings and stables . . . Beyond these buildings was a little narrow town garden with a few poplars, an earwiggy arbour, now and then a dead cat, some empty bottles, and a few articles of personal and domestic use no longer judged to be of house room. The manager of the bank, Mr Calvert, lived in a house he had built on the London road, and used to come to the bank on a little cob, riding it over the pavement and up the paved yard to the stable beyond."

The partners themselves were both hunting men, and occasionally used to come to the office in their scarlet coats, on their way to the meet, or call in afterwards, splashed and tired, to do a little business and sign a few cheques.

Samuel's own hours were very moderate, from nine to four, six days a week. "I learned to be punctual; nine o'clock did not mean the last stroke of the clock, but the first, and to come in after the clock had struck five times was to be late." As junior clerk he had to call at the post office and bring the letters, and unbar the front door of the bank.

"My first duty was to unscrew five nuts, with handles to them, which bound three strong iron bars across the armour-clad door. Then, throwing it back against the wall, I hung on hinges, at the side from which it opened, a light door with glass in the top panel, having the word 'Bank' written in large gilt letters. My next business was to mend the pens; we used nothing but quills, steel pens not being

allowed. Nor had we any gas. When light was needed a number of tin candlesticks, with large bases, were produced and gave a dim light. Our quill box was a curiosity. At one end of the counter was a deep drawer which rolled out on wheels; in this were stored thousands of quills, which lay there to ripen and harden. I was allowed several pen-knives which I kept as sharp as razors and by constant practice I became a very expert pen-maker.

"The pens made, I retired to a back seat, where, with a little board before me, a brush, a saucer of water, some gummed paper, and a heap of old local bank notes, I proceeded to repair and piece the notes so as to fit them for use again.

"Banks used then to issue their own notes, but were limited in the amount of issue, and a declaration had to be made by one of the partners before a commissioner of oaths as to the number issued. They came back to us torn, or in halves, pinned together, or fastened with wafers, and it was my business to turn them out respectable for future use. When past mending they were taken in sealed parcels by one of the partners to a furnace belonging to one of the ironworks and dropped in.

"This work was monotonous and uninspiring, but I got the chance, when we were not very busy, of reading *The Times*. The Crimean War was going on, and I read Russell's accounts of the horrible sufferings endured by our soldiers owing to the frightful mismanagement of the authorities. I remember well the consternation and indignation which pervaded the country. There was also a great agitation about the nursing of the sick and wounded, for the hospitals were dismally deficient in every way."

His other task was to copy the letters by hand into a book before they were dispatched. This had been the custom in all offices since offices began, and when a traveller tried to sell the firm a copying machine the older clerks looked at it with suspicion and contempt. It was bought however, and Samuel put it to such good use and produced such good results that the bank never went back to the old system.

He didn't mind the work, it was the sitting around waiting for it that fretted him sometimes beyond bearing, so that he would seize up his hat and rush out with some excuse – just to get a breath of fresh air. He had a fortnight's holiday a year, but there were no Bank Holidays, and the Saturday half-holiday was not brought in until he had been at the bank for some time. But what he really disliked about his early days as junior clerk was his duty as bank watchdog.

"Adjoining the bank was a dark, dreary room, which gained what light it had from windows looking out on to the passage up the yard. Over the mantelpiece were six flint muskets, a pair of seaman's cutlasses, and a brace of pistols arranged in a kind of 'trophy'. These had been procured and stored at the bank at the time of the Reform Riots in 1832 to protect the place in case of attack.

"In one corner was a cupboard-looking thing, which was in reality a bedstead which let down at night and formed a very uncomfortable resting-place. The room was furnished chiefly with large deed-boxes, having their owner's names in white letters on them, and deposited with us for safety, assured by the blunderbusses and cutlasses and my presence, for here I was condemned to sleep every night.

"The old clerk used to go round the bank with me, try the door of the strong-room, see that the bells were hung on the shutters, look himself into the bank in the dark to see that nothing was on fire, and then I fastened myself into the disused room, with a single candlestick to make the furniture as ghostly as might be. There were shutters over the windows, and the first thing that met one's eyes in the morning were two glaring eyeballs (like Robinson Crusoe's goat) caused by round holes cut into the shutters; through these also the old clerk could see the light of my candle shining on the wall opposite, and know when I put out my light and when I was reading in bed."

This misery he endured for three or four years, when another junior came, and the task was passed on to him. He was not unhappy, though. He had earned £50 for his first year's work, and was proudly conscious that he was the first child in the family to stand on his own feet. He had friends in Derby, and an uncle who was a clergyman there, and he enjoyed the evening parties and the rambles and excursions after work was over. And in the later 1850's he became an enthusiastic member of the 6th Derbyshire Volunteers, giving up his free time to drill and rifle practice. He was a crack marksman, and remembered with grim satisfaction the time when he showed a Government inspector how he could in five shots hit the bulls-eye four times and the centre once. The inspector had grumbled about being late for luncheon, but Samuel had had to go without his altogether.

Then on 26 June, 1860 he and thousands of others travelled up to London for a special review in Hyde Park which the Queen inspected. The bank, somewhat grudgingly, gave him the day off, and he left Derby at 4 o'clock in the morning to arrive in London at 8.00. The bells were ringing in the steeples to mark the occasion, but what he appreciated was the meal that was provided for them when they got out of the station; the lettuces in particular were so crisp and good. There were 20,000 of them there in Hyde Park. They sprawled about in the hot afternoon waiting for the parade to begin and ate sandwiches out of their cartridge cases. The trees were full of little boys and the excitement was intense. At the end of the parade all 20,000 of them cheered the Queen, the officers waving their swords and the men brandishing their rifles.

But by the following year he was beginning to have serious thoughts of leaving the bank and going into the Church. His prospects in Derby were good; he was earning £130 a year, and he was advancing, whereas it was difficult to know how he could finance himself as a student; his father could give little help. In the end an old friend

SCENE AT THE VOLUNTEER REVIEW IN HYDE PARK.

of the family offered £50 a year for two years, and he set to in good earnest to teach himself enough to matriculate at Cambridge. It meant taking up Greek and Latin again at the point he had thankfully abandoned them eight years before. For a year he never spent an evening away from his books, and used to get up early in the morning and pace the streets of Derby chanting Greek irregular verbs.

And thus in October, 1863 began what Samuel Scott called his no.3 life – at Trinity College, Cambridge.

Rookes and Evelyn

TWO MIDSHIPMEN AT SEBASTOPOL

I N Derby Samuel Scott sat in the bank and read *The Times*. "The winter of 1854–55 was the terrible winter of the Crimean War. Every one was made miserable by the accounts of the awful sufferings of our soldiers and sailors in the trenches before Sebastopol. The suspense became intolerable; from September, 1854 to September, 1855, the dismal strife went on, and for what?"

It was forty years after the Napoleonic Wars, when England had almost forgotten the miseries and only remembered the victories, and most of her generals knew more about parades and reviews than about active service, that the Crimean War was fought on the heights of a peninsula in the Black Sea, burning hot and fly-ridden in the summer, a bleak and desolate waste in the winter. There was a new enemy, Russia, and after centuries of war with France the generals had to accustom themselves to be linked with her now as an ally.

The bravely-dressed army, whom Mary Howitt had seen in 1853 on a sunny Surrey common, were in just over a year half naked and shivering. Nobody foresaw this, least of all the troops themselves, who were raring to be off and have a swipe at the Russians. The Cromptons, when they parted with their turbulent son in 1854, surely did not know where the child would be taken. Admittedly the boy was getting out of hand, and the English upper classes traditionally feel that only the maximum discomfort and a parting from their families at a tender age can make men of their sons, but even so it would be unusual deliberately to expose a ten-year-old to trench warfare in Crimean conditions.

The father was an officer in the West Yorkshire Light Infantry Militia, and had been posted to Gibraltar. The whole family had gone with him, and young Rookes Evelyn Bell Crompton (these were all family names) had become rather a problem. He seems to have been a cheerful, cocky little boy, without a nerve in his body, a pest to his seniors and to his contemporaries, but likeable never-theless. Very much the same as John Shipp, in fact. In Gibraltar he worried his family by going off adventuring on his pony into Spain and into Morocco, and he was thoroughly spoilt by the garrison.

And then a lucky chance arose. His mother's cousin, a naval captain in command of H.M.S. *Dragon*, a sailing ship fitted with auxiliary steam machinery (a very recent innovation in the navy),

MIDSHIPMEN'S BERTH

called in at Gibraltar on the way to the Crimea. He agreed to take the boy on board. After only a couple of days of his nephew's company he too had had enough. Master Crompton was removed from the captain's quarters and set to work with the cadets, under the supervision of the ship's Instructor. Even in those days when education of naval officers started so young, he was well below the age of the youngest on board. Still, he does not seem to have been daunted, and in the reminiscences that he wrote seventy years later, he remembered the whole trip with the greatest satisfaction. For one thing, he commanded the captain's gig, and had a splendid time shouting orders at a crew of sailors old enough to be his father. Exciting things happened on the way; they towed a stranded troopship at Malta, visited the Valley of Sweet Waters at Constantinople, and towed another ship, a sailing vessel laden with military stores, across the Black Sea to Balaclava, running into a stiff storm.

At Balaclava he somehow managed to get permission to go ashore and visit his brother in the trenches dug in front of the Russian fortifications round Sebastopol. It was just before the attack on the fortification known as the Redan, which was only taken with frightful slaughter. Master Crompton, who was not imaginative or sensitive, had only one comment to make – about how the ground in front of the trenches seemed to be strewn with blue gravel, but he found it was all spent bullets. Because of his experiences, even though they were short, he was later awarded the Crimean Medal and the Sebastopol Clasp. It must have made him a very difficult subject to squash when he went back to England and a more normal education the following year, and he said in his memoirs that he got into trouble for treating senior boys at his prep school, and later at Harrow, as though they were his inferiors.

But it was not just the luck of being in the Crimean trenches at the age of ten that makes Rookes Evelyn Bell Crompton (who was later to become an electrical engineer of great distinction) of interest. With great good fortune he found himself in the Navy at the moment of transition between sail and steam. And the fortune does not seem to have been on his side only; at ten years old, *he* managed to help the Navy come to terms with this daunting new machinery.

"I was a precocious boy, and already keenly and intelligently interested in anything to do with mechanics. At that time engines and boilers had only been recently introduced into Her Majesty's ships, and most of the steam machinery was auxiliary. The line-of-battle ships were fitted with screws mounted in cages or carriages, which could slide up and down in a vertical well, placed just in front of the rudder-post, and the screws were only lowered into position and attached to the propellor-shaft when the wind fell and the sails could no longer be used. I believe I was the only member of my mess who took the trouble to learn about the engines of the *Dragon* and of the Admiral's ship, the *Hannibal*. They used to come to me for explanations of mechanical matters, and I was able on one occasion to be of use to an officer of higher rank. Captain Robb of the *Caesar* was expecting a visit of inspection from the Admiral, and was conscious of being rather 'shaky' on the subject of his engines. He got me to prime him on matters of horsepower, steaming capacity and the like, and was able to answer the Admiral's inquiries correctly."

How very daunting for a Harrow prefect to try to snub a veteran with this sort of experience!

Young Crompton might swagger around at Harrow, but he was not a Crimean veteran in the way that Evelyn Wood was, who fought in the trenches in front of Sebastopol, and was recommended for the Victoria Cross, at the age of sixteen.

He had passed into the Navy as a cadet when he was fourteen. The entrance test does not seem to have been very exacting – he spoke in his memoirs of some history questions and a dictation. But there must have been some way of weeding out the weaklings, because the Navy asked a great deal of its cadets. You had to be, if not fearless, then able to hide your fear, and shin up rigging at the double and reef the topsails a hundred or more feet from deck in half a gale. Discipline was ferocious. He was seen loafing with his hands in his pockets a few weeks after his arrival on board.

"Most Captains would have been sufficiently preoccupied to disregard a small boy. Not so, however, was our Chief. . . 'What are you doing, sir, with hands in pockets? Aft here, sail-maker's mate, with needle and tar.' A big hairy seaman came aft with his needle and tar bucket. 'Sew this young gentleman's hands up in his pockets.' I was seized, but as the first stitch was put in the Captain said, 'Not this time, but if I see your hands there again, there they'll be for a week.'"

The standard punishment was "watch and watch", which meant four hours on watch and four hours off throughout the whole twenty-four hours with all your normal duties thrown in as well. Evelyn did a stint of this for three unbroken weeks before the ship's doctor interfered. Responsibility came early – even small boys were put in charge of the crew of a cutter and made to deal with the drunken escapades of seamen on shore leave, and by the time Evelyn was sixteen he was supervising the punishment of a hundred and fifty mutinous men, and seeing that they in their turn kept "watch and watch".

It was the year that he passed the midshipman's exam that the British fleet, cruising in the Black Sea, heard that war had been declared on Russia. Officers and men were all spoiling for the fight, and they gave three cheers for war, which were echoed by their French and Turkish allies. It was very disappointing to them all that there was no immediate action, and life went on much as before, with the midshipmen skylarking and playing follow-my-leader up and down the rigging (Evelyn was nearly killed when he fell from it once), and regattas organized to while away the time.

Then that August, 1853, everybody was sobered. Cholera broke out in the fleet. The army camps on the mainland were already full of it; the war was becoming more than just reviews and regattas. Cholera was a terrifying disease, sudden and violent. "The screams of a sufferer when seized with cramp often brought on other seizures, and the scenes on a middle or lower deck were trying even to strong nerves." The Navy was far better equipped to fight the disease – and indeed, as Evelyn Wood says throughout the Memoirs, better organized in every way, particularly as regards the men's comfort – but in the close quarters of a ship the infection burst with the force of an explosive. The English flagship lost one tenth of its crew, and in a few days some of the ships, from a crew of seven hundred to a thousand, were so reduced that they had not enough men to work the sails.

That was Evelyn's first taste of what the Crimean campaign was going to be like. The next was a few weeks later, when parties of sailors landed to bury the dead after the battle of Alma. "We buried over seven hundred bodies in and around the breastwork where the most determined struggle occured." These were men whom the Navy had landed a few days earlier, the sailors very often carrying the soldiers, who were weak with cholera and encumbered with full-dress uniform and gaudy head-dresses, through the shallows.

But he was still straining for action. On 1 October, when he was on duty as Signal Midshipman of the watch, he took a message: "Line-of-battle ships will send a hundred and forty men and proportion of officers for service with land forces." He could hardly hope to be sent; there were other midshipmen senior to him, but when he went to the quarterdeck where the Captain and the Commander were selecting the officers he was trembling with excitement.

The Captain was in fact Evelyn's uncle, and though a kindly man, treated his nephew with special severity – afraid, no doubt, of being accused of favouritism. But on this occasion he had made up his mind that the family was going to be represented in the fighting.

"The Captain said: 'Which midshipman?'
'I am thinking, sir!'
'Take young Wood.'
'Oh! he's too young, sir. It will kill him!'
'No, Burnett. I'll answer for him.'
And as the Commander said, 'Well, youngster, you shall come,' I felt I could never sufficiently repay my uncle."

The next day the naval contingent began to haul their guns up the steep cliffs from Balaclava Plain – the cliffs that were to make life so fearful in the coming winter for those camped above, waiting for food and supplies to struggle up to them. They found themselves on a gaunt, bare plateau, cut by ravines, dropping down at the further end to Sebastopol harbour. On ridges above the harbour the Russians had built their fortifications, and opposite them were the Allied trenches and artillery, including the naval gun batteries.

It was in these trenches that the French and the British armies were to live and fight and suffer for so many weary months. Few people foresaw how long the siege would be,

"On the 16th of October bets were freely offered in our camp that the city would fall in twenty-four hours. Some of the older and more prudent officers gave the Russians forty-eight hours, but no one thought they could withstand our fire longer. My older messmates would not allow me to buy a good Paris-made gold watch which a soldier had taken at the Alma and offered to sell for £1,

for they said, 'In forty-eight hours gold watches will be much cheaper!' When orders were issued that afternoon detailing Lieutenant Partridge and Mr Sanctuary for the first or daylight relief of the *Queen's*, Lieutenant Douglas and Mr Wood for the second relief at 10 a.m., Douglas swore, and I cried from vexation, so persuaded were we all that the Russians would offer but little resistance after four hours' bombardment."

Evelyn Wood left a grim account of that terrible winter spent in front of Sebastopol; a winter in which the British soldiers turned from bravely-dressed peacocks into gaunt, half-starved, half-naked scarecrows. Everything failed them: their officers, supplies, shelter, food, medical attention – everything except their own courage and cheerfulness. The sailors, with far more resourceful officers and imaginative organization, managed infinitely better. Their tents were dry, their clothes were adequate, their health was looked after, they had hot food prepared for them by their own cooks, while the soldiers – or those who had enough strength – were grubbing for vine roots to boil themselves a little coffee.

183

Evelyn – he was Field Marshal Sir Evelyn Wood by the time he came to write his memoirs – dwelt more on the sufferings of the soldiers than of his own during that winter of 1854–5, but they must have been considerable. He had always felt the cold acutely. He was not naturally fearless – he was often frightened during the midshipmen's wild games in the rigging. He never got used to being under fire; he could only forget the shots whistling past and the shells bursting if he was concentrating on something else. From this point of view, he said, it was easiest if you were one of a gun's crew, because there you were in a team working together. He was with his gun battery one day, and, having just been relieved, was settling down to enjoy his salt pork ration and milkless tea, when a Russian shell set the roof of the powder magazine on fire. The officer who had relieved him lost his head, the men panicked, and Evelyn, furious at the interruption and the way the sand had showered over his pork, put down his meal, stamped on the fire, and put out the rest of the

AMBULANCE TRANSPORT SERVICE

flames by squatting on them. For this he was recommended for the V.C. when it was instituted a year later.*

It was 16 October, 1854, when he wept with vexation because he thought Sebastopol would be taken before he had a chance to go into action, and 20 June, 1855 that he was carried, wounded, on to his uncle's ship, H.M.S. *Queen*, and thence transferred to a ship back to England.

It was not his superior officer's fault that Evelyn was wounded, for he had done his best to keep the boy away from the assault that was impending on the Redan. Evelyn had been ill and feverish with severe intestinal trouble and had been living on tinned milk and rice for a week. Even so, he was desperate to be included in the naval contingent that was taking part. Captain Peel, who was commanding, said he might go as far as the gun battery, and no further, and told the sentry on duty privately that the boy was not to be woken up when the assault parties paraded. But Michael Hardy, one of the sailors, shook him awake.

"I told him to go away, as I was too ill to move, to which he replied, 'Shure, you'll never forgive yourself if you miss this morning's fun;' and against my will he proceeded to dress me. It did not take long, for my attire consisted of cap, jacket, trousers, and shoes. Hardy having propped me up against the tent-pole, brought my pony, on which he put me, being obliged, however, to hold me in the saddle, for I was too weak to grip with my legs. We hurried after the men for two miles down to the trenches as fast as darkness permitted, and soon after 1 a.m. reached the 21-gun battery, where I tied the pony to a Lancaster gun."

The battery at 2 a.m. was a scene of wild confusion. The officers were organizing the men into parties – six men to each of the eighteen-foot ladders with which it was hoped to scale the Redan fortifications – trying to keep them quiet, looking for Engineers who were supposed to guide the assault troops. Captain Peel, to Evelyn's great irritation, kept trying to invent useless errands to keep the boy away from the attack, but at last gave up, and he was put in charge of a ladder party.

The Redan fortifications consisted of two faces seventy yards long and some seventeen feet high which met at an angle. To reach these

* He did not receive it then, but as a result of action in India later.

THE REDAN AT SUNRISE, SEPTEMBER 9. – REMOVING THE WOUNDED

the assault party would have to cross slopes of rank grass, treacherous
with old gravel pits, shell holes, and trenches – quarter of a mile of
open ground, encumbered with their heavy ladders and all the time
exposed to heavy fire from the Russians. Then they would be faced
by the abatis – an outer defence about five feet high and four wide,
made of felled trees and brushwood. Beyond this was another
stretch of open ground, then a deep and wide ditch, on the further
side of which were the Russians, high on the Redan, ranged four or
six men deep, firing down at the English and calling on them sar-
castically to walk in. From the bottom of the ditch to the top of the
parapet where the Russians were standing was a height of twenty feet.

The party which hoped to take this position consisted of two
columns of a hundred riflemen to lead the way, then twelve engineers, followed by fifty soldiers carrying sacks of wool and hay to fill
the ditches, then the ladder parties (sixty sailors and sixty soldiers),
and finally four hundred men who were to storm the fortifications.
The Redan assault was, from the start, a fearful mistake, but Lord
Raglan, the Commander-in-Chief, felt it his duty to try to divert
Russian fire from the French who were suffering appalling losses

as they attacked another part of the Sebastopol defences. And the
men too were as eager as Midshipman Wood for the attack.

As the sailors stood by waiting for the signal, a shell fell into the
storming party and blew up a soldier. Evelyn, taking his eyes off the
body as it fell, saw the signal flag being run up, and shouting "Flag's
up", jumped on to the little bank which had sheltered them.
Captain Peel behind him, waving his sword in the dim light, shouted
"Come on, sailors; don't let the soldiers beat you."

From the first moments, the fire from the Redan parapets was
murderous. An officer standing near Lord Raglan and watching the
masses of Russians who opposed the little body of English said
"There is no hope for them." In his memoirs Evelyn Wood said that
the shower of missiles pattered on the ground like tropical rain when
the monsoon breaks, and then would come "death-dealing gusts of
increased density, which swept down the hill, felling our men as a
reaping-machine levels standing crops."

But Evelyn was on fire with excitement; he had been too weak to
sit on his pony without support when he went down to the battery,
now he ran on in front of the ladder parties.

"Before we had gone a hundred yards, several sailors were struck
down, and I was hit by a bullet while cheering on the Bluejackets
and waving my sword, which was knocked five yards away from me.
My arm was paralysed by the jar, and I thought it was off, as I
instinctively dropped on one knee. On looking down, I saw it was
only a flesh wound of the hand, and jumped up hastily, fearing that
anyone passing might think I was skulking. Picking up my sword, I
found it was twisted like a corkscrew, so threw it down, and with it
the scabbard, which had got between my legs. I had no pistol, and
thus was without any weapon, but that did not occur to my mind as I
ran on to overtake the leading ladder."

By the time they had covered two hundred and fifty yards, or
about half the distance to the abatis, he was the only naval officer
left on his feet. The ladder bearers had fallen too; of the ten ladders
that had started, only one got within twenty-five yards of the abatis,
with two men to it, a young seaman in front and Evelyn himself
behind. The seaman turned his head, and not recognizing the midshipman called back, "Come along, Bill, let's get our beggar up
first." And then he was killed, and with him tumbled the ladder. "In

my heart I experienced a sense of relief, from the feeling that my responsibility was over, as even my most gallant Chief, William Peel, would not expect me to carry a ladder eighteen feet in length by myself."

On the parapets the Russians were shouting down taunts, but there were few people to hear them. Evelyn saw a young sergeant trying to get men to follow him through the abatis, and shouting that he would shoot the man next to him if he did not follow. The private looked deliberately on the hundreds of Russians above them, and then at the pitiful remnant of the English, and refused. As the sergeant brought his rifle on his shoulder to fire he was hit by grape-shot, and dropped dead. Crouching in the shelter of the abatis, Evelyn was asking an army officer about the chance of getting through when that man too was hit and lay screaming with a stomach wound, calling on his mother, to Evelyn's great distress. He was walking along the abatis, looking for a place where he might clamber over when case shot came crashing through it and smashed his arm, knocking him to the ground unconscious.

"I do not know how long I was unconscious, but it cannot have been many minutes; for the whole affair did not last more than half an hour. I was aroused by an Irish corporal, who shook my arm, saying, 'Matey, if you are going in, you had better go at once, or you'll get bayoneted.' I presume it was the pain in my arm which brought me back to consciousness, but I answered the man with an outburst of bad language. He drew himself up erect, and bringing his hand across his body to the rifle said, 'I beg your pardon, sir, I did not know you were an officer. Can I help you?'"

Helped to his feet, Evelyn followed the sergeant towards the English lines, but weak and faint he could only go slowly. At one point he stepped down into a shallow ditch which gave a little shelter from the Russian fire, but the screams of wounded men, trampled on by their fleeing comrades – for the Retire had now been sounded – sent him out again. Trying to find a lower place in the four-foot English parapet where he could get over without so much effort, he was jostled out of his place by a young soldier. "A round shot passing over my right shoulder struck him between the shoulders, and I stepped over the remains of his body so exhausted as to be indifferent to his death and to my preservation." There was

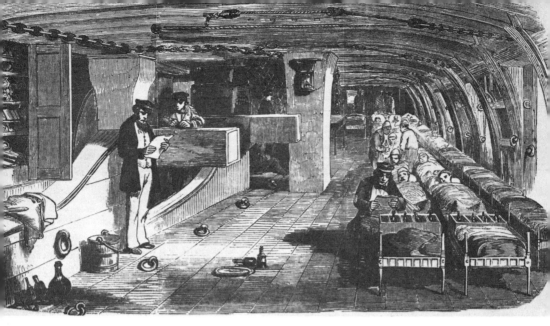

THE SICK-DECK OF "THE BELLEISLE" HOSPITAL-SHIP IN FARO SOUND

still the parapet of the gun battery to climb, and he faltered when it came to jumping down, terrified of jarring his arm. A sergeant shouted at him: "Jump, jump, you little devil, or you will get killed."

Two officers carried him over the parapet and he was taken to an Irish doctor who greeted him warmly. "Sit down, my dear boy, an' I'll have your arm off before you know where you are." Evelyn resisted, weak as he was. Eventually he was put on a stretcher and carried to camp.

"Whilst waiting in the operating-tent for my turn for the table, I was interested by the extraordinary fortitude of a Bluejacket, who discussed the morning's failure without a break in his voice while the doctors were removing two of his fingers at the third joint. When my turn came, I had a heated argument with the surgeons, who wished to amputate the arm above the elbow. The Navy had then an officer dangerously ill from a wound received a few days earlier, in which case amputation had been delayed too long, and all but the senior Doctor wished to take off my arm. To him I appealed to be allowed the chance, and to persuade him I underwent considerable pain. . . . I doubling my fist raised the arm as high as I could, until the case-shot met the fore and upper arm, on which the senior Medical officer decided that he would at all events try to save the limb."

The limb was saved; the shot was removed under an anaesthetic, which in those very early days meant that a chloroform-soaked handkerchief was put on his face. It was a severe injury, and the bone had splintered (he later removed eight needle-like pieces himself, using a mirror, as he had "always been a nervous patient under a surgeon"), and he was sent back to his ship. The Commander of the Naval Brigade wrote to his uncle.

"Camp before Sebastopol.
18th June, 10.30 a.m.

MY DEAR MICHELL. You will be sorry to hear your young nephew, Wood, has been wounded by a grapeshot in the arm. The shot struck the bone obliquely, and was cut out when he got into camp. I saw him in the trenches, and he bore it like a hero. He was Peel's A.D.C., and Peel endeavoured to keep the boy from the murderous fire into which they plunged with the scaling ladders, but he would take no refusal, and went with the rest. Wood will be at Kazatch today in Lord Raglan's carriage. Will you have a boat? Yours, in haste, STEPHEN LUSHINGTON"

It was, of course, a mark of enormous favour to be taken down to the boat in the Commander-in-Chief's own carriage, and three days later, Evelyn asked his uncle to write to Lord Raglan in his name to thank him. A reply came that same day.

"MY DEAR CAPTAIN MICHELL, I am very glad to have had an opportunity of being even in the smallest degree useful to your nephew, whose distinguished career cannot fail to enlist everybody in his favour. I am rejoiced to hear that he is going on well. Believe me, very faithfully yours, RAGLAN."

Five days later Lord Raglan himself was taken ill. Infinitely grieved by the uselessness of this last attack, by the slaughter of 1,500 of his men in a campaign which had lost England some 20,000 lives, he sunk into death without resistance. Evelyn Wood wrote of him fifty years later: "He was one of the most uncomplaining, loyal servants the British nation ever had; ordered by the Government to carry out a difficult task with inadequate means, he died from care and overwhelming anxiety, a victim to England's unreadiness for war."

Evelyn was young and resilient. No sooner had his parents got him home but he was pestering them to return him – not as a midshipman this time, but as a soldier, and on 1st January, 1856, Cornet Evelyn Wood, of the 13th Light Dragoons, marched out of the barracks at Dorchester, on his way for the second time to the Crimea.

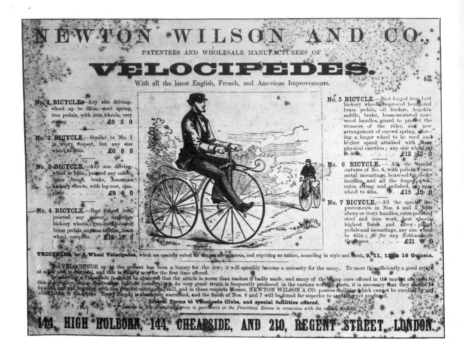

Henrietta

GREAT EVENTS AT WINCHMORE HILL

WILLIAM HOWITT had watched "ever-devouring London, as it crept ever nearer," and had been saddened at the way it trampled down the countryside that he loved. A girl called Henrietta, in the Middlesex village of Winchmore Hill, watched the railway arrive in her pleasant valley in 1869 and turn it into just another North London suburb. Half a century later, to make money for a bazaar, she wrote down her memories of those far-off days (referring to herself in the third person, as 'Winifred'), and it was published under the title of *Winchmore Hill, Memories of a Lost Village*. By that time, 1912, it was just a part of London; in William Howitt's words, "the tide of population had rolled on with bricks and mortar in its rear."

For nearly ten years before its first sod was turned the villagers had spoken of "when the railway comes," and "if the railway comes." Various plans were discussed, but as nothing came of them, most people felt they would not believe in the railway until they saw it. To Henrietta Cresswell the small happenings of the village were much more important than the vast world of London that lay somewhere to the south, and the villagers thought more about the passing seasons and the events of the farming year than they did about the Crimean War and the Indian Mutiny. News arrived by the mid-day omnibus, and great events were shouted by the driver as he passed, but they made little stir in the quiet valley. Henrietta's father was the doctor there, and he often came back from his rounds with his tall stove-pipe hat full of mushrooms that he had picked in a field, or with roses or pinks in it that he had been given from a cottage garden.

Natural events like the great hailstorm which broke all the glass-houses in the village, killed cattle, and shattered windows did rouse the villagers. So did the comet of 1858. They had known about its coming from Old Moore's Almanack, and many of them had dreaded it, thinking that it surely meant great disaster would follow. But Henrietta remembered it as a supremely beautiful sight, although she was only three when it crossed those summer skies.

Her uncle had spent the day with them, and Henrietta and her mother had walked part of the way towards London with him.

"They halted on the Kings Arms bridge over the New River to say goodbye. It was a lovely evening – the sky amber and aquamarine. Grey mists were creeping up from the winding silver ribbon of water, and the willow-shrouded banks of Pym's brook. The dark yew trees made a black mass in front of the weird old white house known as Bowes Farm, and contrasted with the bright afterglow in the Western sky.

"The scene was peace itself. The silence was only broken by the last chipper of a bird in the elm trees or the splash of a fish jumping in the river, but above and beyond all else, dominating the light, the silence and the landscape, was the first sight of the great Comet, small as yet, and appearing as a bright star and a strange, ever widening beam of light paling the planets by contrast. That was the first time Winifred saw it, but after, night by night, it grew till half the sky seemed full of the glory of it, and then when it had become part of her young life, it decreased as it had increased and was gone. The village was left with only the Comet year as a date to reckon by.

Many regarded it with awe, and even with terror, but no memory of it remained to Winifred in after life so distinct as that of the first sight of its glory, over the fields, the stream, and the slow flowing river on that night so long ago."

The next year, 1859, was another great year for Winchmore Hill, and was known as "the year of the Fancy Fair." Money was needed to build a school, for the one-roomed cottage that they had used up till now was far too small for modern requirements, and was going to be replaced by a National School.

The Fair was held in a neighbouring park. It was the greatest festivity Henrietta had ever known, and she wore a new hat and drove quite a long way in the village fly, through the lodge gates and up the avenue to the open ground where the tents had all been erected. There were flags, a band playing, and crowds of people and carriages and horses.

The village had worked hard to stock all the stalls. Henrietta's father had written verses for the occasion, and painted views of the village on top of sheets of writing paper. His sister had done quantities of embroidered wool work, including a whole set of dinner mats. "Winifred became the happy possessor of a real live Jack-in-the-box. A box covered with marbled paper and a Jack with a fiery red beard. Her mother, on the second day, when things became cheap, bought a pair of ormolu candlesticks with crystal drops that could be unhung and held up to the light for you to look through the prisms and see all the colours of the rainbow. They were a joy for many a day."

Great pride was taken in the yellow brick school buildings when they were finished that year. There was a school hall sixty feet long with a high timbered roof and two fireplaces to warm it, a large infant school with galleries, spacious classrooms, and large play-grounds. There was a grand concert to celebrate the opening of the school, which was decorated with wreaths of evergreens and mottoes of leaves on scarlet flannel backgrounds which the four-year-old Henrietta, too young for the concert, had helped to sew.

The village was proud, too, of the doctor and his brother-in-law in their uniform of the 33rd Middlesex Rifle Volunteers – a grey cloth tunic and trousers, trimmed with narrow red braid, their peaked caps surmounted by a plume of black and scarlet horsehair. The country's unprepared state for the Crimean War after forty

THE FANCY FAIR.

peaceful years, and the Indian Mutiny in 1857 had jolted the public, and in the years that followed corps of Volunteers were formed. There was one at Tottenham, five miles away, and the doctor and his brother-in-law used to take the Red Omnibus or walk there to attend the drills and firing practice. The Volunteers were known as "Her Majesty's Mixed Pins" because of their difference in height, and one of them was caricatured in *Punch* because he had to stand on a felled tree to reach to load his rifle which was the old-fashioned muzzle-loading sort. But Henrietta thought it was all splendid. She could not lift her father's rifle, but she learnt her drill from him with a little old rusty fowling piece, and he painted her a real target to shoot at with her bows and arrows. She stitched red braid on an old grey jacket to wear in imitation of him, and later her best dress was trimmed with Austrian knots to look like his coat. Her father went to represent the 33rd Middlesex at shooting competitions, but Henrietta remembered these not so much for the honour of having a father who was a crack shot, but for the plants that he brought home from Wimbledon Common – plants like sundew and cotton grass, that did not grow at Winchmore Hill.

She was always to remember, too, "the cart on the green." Its arrival was something of a mystery at first, a well-to-do vehicle quite different from a gipsy's caravan. The horse was led away to the inn stables and not turned loose to graze, so it looked as though the cart had come to stay. There was a door in the side, and the cart seemed

to be divided into two parts, one lit by a skylight, and the other quite dark. The village puzzled over it, and then next day they saw frames of portraits on each side of the doorway, and a list of prices. It was a Photographic Establishment, and everybody flocked to be taken. It was a lengthy business; the exposures lasted fully half a minute; no wonder the effort to look pleasant resulted in a furious scowl or a fixed grin.

"Winifred was dressed in her best black silk frock, with a saucer neck and short puffed sleeves, and her coral necklace, and went with her father to be photographed. She was given a rose to hold in her hand, and solemnly gazed into the camera for what seemed an unending space of time, rigidly endeavouring to hold her breath and not move a muscle till the cap was safely back upon the lens.

"Then the photographer departed into his inner chamber. There were mysterious sounds of running water and splashings, combined with a strong aroma of ether which filled the air and gave her a light-headed sensation. Presently the man returned with a dripping plate, backed with black paint, on which was her portrait in various shades of greenish grey. It was pronounced a success, and she again underwent the ordeal in another position. The next day the photographs were fetched home, finished and perfect, each in an oval frame with four gilt corners, surrounded by a piping of crimson velvet, and a square outer case of brownish purple leather paper."

The sight of a velocipede ridden down the hill made the same sort of sensation in Winchmore Hill. The local people called it a "philosopher", the nearest they could get to the word. It was a cumbrous vehicle on four wooden wheels, and when Henrietta's father had looked it over he shook his head and said "It was all very well for people to try and make self-propelled vehicles, but they were never likely to succeed, because while a man was moving a carriage in which he was seated he must always incur the fatigue of carrying his own weight plus that of the machine, and that could never be borne for any length of time or with much rapidity of motion."

But he lived to buy a tricycle, and to see the roads full of wheels.

"The first tricycle the Doctor purchased weighed about 120 lbs., and carried two riders back to back, and, in his case, a white Pomeranian dog, who found plenty of room between the two; the pedals

The Social.

were on long levers with direct action, and the leg motion extra-ordinary. The driving wheel was five feet in diameter and was on one side, while there were two very small wheels on the other. The rims were extremely narrow, and the solid rubber tyres were cemented in, and were continually becoming partly or wholly detached. The seat was a large flat platform of metal, and had a blue cloth cushion like a carriage seat mattressed with *hard buttons*, which was fastened on by a leather strap and buckle. The steering was effected by a long lever acting on the foremost of the little side wheels, a mere touch taking vast effect.

"Perhaps the most primitive portion of the whole machine was the brake, which was simply a bar of iron, raised and lowered by means of a chain, which dragged on the ground and checked the pace of the tricycle by digging its end into the gravel. Notwithstanding its many shortcomings, it was very fast, and when two passengers were on board the fatigue of riding was comparatively small."

But a faster vehicle yet was on its way to Winchmore Hill. In the summer of 1869, one that was later to be remembered for its heat and drought, a load of barrows, shovels and tip trucks arrived in the valley, a few sods were ceremoniously turned in a large field, and work was begun on the new branch line that was to extend the Great Northern Railway to Hertford. In a few days rows of wooden huts had sprung up, and gangs of navvies were in possession.

The village had dreaded those navvies. Fearful stories had been told of their lawless way of life, their hard drinking, thieving and rioting, and the way they could devastate the area of the country where they were working with the law helpless. It was true that navvies were not regarded as such savage monsters as they had been before the fifties. The public had had time to get used to them, and they had won honour and respect in the Crimean War for the way they had got down to building the Balaclava railway. But Winchmore Hill did not know what to expect of this army that the contractor was bringing from Yorkshire and Lincolnshire. On the whole their conduct was very orderly, much to everybody's relief, and they certainly behaved very well when they were near the doctor's house. Many of the navvies brought their food or their tea cans to be heated on the great kitchen range, and one of them, "Dandy Ganger", a burly man decorated with many large mother-of-pearl buttons and a big silver watch chain, made sure that there was no bad language used anywhere near the house.

It was the railway itself that made such devastation. The valley had to be spanned between the village and the hills to the north. Clay and gravel were excavated to fill parts of it, embankments were thrown up, the streams were imprisoned in culverts, bridge after bridge was built, either to carry rail over road or road over rail; there was a viaduct.

"The pretty row of cottages where the Grandmother lived were pulled down, the great ash arbour ruthlessly destroyed, and the garden devastated; the holly hedge, dense as a wall, was grubbed up, scarcely anything remained but the tall yew and a golden-knob apple tree, which for years after blossomed and fruited, on the top of the cutting by Vicarsmoor Bridge. The lane was closed for traffic,

and a notice board proclaimed, 'This Road is stopped time the Bridge is being built.'

"The excavations were beautiful in colour, the London clay being a bright cobalt blue when first cut through, and changing with exposure to orange. There were strata of black and white flints and yellow gravel; the men's white slops and the red heaps of burnt ballast made vivid effects of light and shade and colour against the cloudless sky of that excessively hot summer. There were also dark wooden planks and shorings to add neutral tints, and when the engine came the glitter of brass and clouds of white steam were added to the landscape. On Sundays and holidays the men were, many of them, resplendent in scarlet or yellow or blue plush waist-coats and knee breeches.

"It was not till 1 January, 1870, that the Doctor's house was given over to the invaders and he moved to Grove Lodge. It was then all deep snow, and the cutting was so close to the side of the house that the garden shrubs were constantly slipping over the edge and having to be brought back and replanted. A portion of the wall was built, but the frost got into the mortar and it fell almost immediately, so the garden became a thoroughfare for the navvies to their work."

The Winchmore Hill section only involved five miles of line, but it was a very difficult stretch, and five navvies were killed in the laying of it. It had been hoped to finish the line in 1870, but work dragged on. The engineers had not believed the inhabitants when they spoke of "lakes of flood water and bridges washed away". They had started work in an unusually dry summer, and when the winter rains came the stream rose alarmingly and cracked the culvert that was supposed to carry it. The blue clay of the valley sank lower and lower until what had been meant for a level line became a steep gradient, and long after the line was open the "slip" as it was called was so dangerous that every train slowed down to pass it, and many people were afraid to travel over it.

There was also, Henrietta remembered, another disaster. A gentleman (perhaps it was her father, though she did not give him away) moved the stumps which marked the line of the railway as it was to pass through his kitchen garden. He never admitted what he had done, but it threw all the surveyor's calculations awry.

All through 1870 the navvies laboured and it seemed as though they had always been there. Now that some track was laid they could use engines to help the men and their barrows. Henrietta more than forty years later remembered those engines and how each had a separate voice.

"*Fox* informed the world there was 'such a hurry, such a hurry." *Hunslet*, a tank engine, was particularly clear in her enunciation,

informing all the world of her huffy temper, though I never heard she was ill to deal with as a worker – 'I'm in a huff, I'm in a huff!' she puffed on her way along the line. *Progress*, who laboured at the Wood Green end, proclaimed continually the name of the chief engineer – 'Mr Claringbull, Mr Claringbull,' she shouted with a strong accent on the last syllable. *Ferret* seldom left the Enfield portion of roadmaking, perhaps because everything was 'such a heavy load, such a heavy load'."

WINCHMORE HILL STATION C 1900

Sometimes, even though the railway was not finished, she had a taste of what it was going to be like when she had a ride back home from the London end on *Fox*, with the little engine bucketing along the roughly laid lines with no weight of trucks behind to steady it.

More ballast was burned for the permanent way, and heavy rails began to take the place of the temporary lines. The winter of 1870 went by and it was said that the line would be open early in the year. Then a definite date was given – the 1st April! The village laughed, but they had to believe when they saw the printed notices. On 31

March, 1871 the navvies celebrated the completion of the line, and the departure of the last train of trucks, with a tremendous fusillade of exploding fog-signals which brought the villagers scurrying down to see what had happened. And then the trucks and the navvies departed, and Winchmore Hill was left with its new station, smelling strongly of fresh paint.

At first traffic on the railway was only a small matter. There were sixteen trains each way daily, and four on Sundays, and the whole station staff consisted of stationmaster, a boy booking-clerk, two signalmen, and a lad porter. By the end of the year there was a telegraph office, though there were rarely more than three messages a day and the messengers spent most of their time delivering groceries. But the whole aspect of the valley had been changed by that army of men with their barrows and their shovels, and where the doctor's house and garden had stood was now a railway bridge. House and garden had vanished; iron girders spanned a cutting where they had stood. But for one or two years after they had been swallowed up "the cutting each summer was a forest of rose and carnation poppies at least three feet high; they revelled in a new soil and made gigantic blossoms in every shade of crimson, scarlet, white, purple, and grey."

Then they too were gone. The leafy lanes, the woods with their cuckoos, the quiet farmlands, all became a thing of the past.

Frederic

THE LORD LIEUTENANT'S SON

THE 1860's: London is galloping towards Winchmore Hill, Samuel Scott is beginning his no.3 life, and we are among the mid-Victorians. Lord Frederic Hamilton (born in 1856) and his brother Ernest, two years younger, always referred to themselves as mid-Victorians, and from the 1920's when they wrote their reminiscences, used to look back on those remote years with a mixture of impatience and affection. Mid-Victorian high society could be dull, and conversation stuffy and the rich disgustingly idle, but there seemed also to be a steadiness and a conscientiousness about the 'mid-Vics' as the Hamiltons called them, which was missing in the giddy post-war years of their old age.

They came at the tail-end of the 2nd Marquis of Abercorn's large family of six sons and seven daughters, and their childhood was by no means dull, stuffy or idle. Lord Abercorn (he was later to be made Duke) owned estates in the north of Ireland, as well as a large

London house, and he took his family to various other houses besides these. Frederic and Ernest, if we are to believe their memoirs, seem to have made the most of their opportunities wherever they were staying, France or England, Scotland or Ireland.

Like Mary Howitt, Frederic Hamilton was fascinated by links with the past. By the time he was born she was fifty-seven. Mary remembered the Napoleonic Wars and George III's jubilee; he recalled with pride that his mother, born in 1812, was in her old age the last person living who had seen George III driving through London, in one of his rare lucid intervals. She had also at the age of twelve danced a Spanish shawl dance for George IV at Brighton Pavilion. The King was delighted, told her she was a pretty little girl, and asked if there was anything he could do for her. "Yes, there is," the child answered, "your Majesty can fetch me some ham sandwiches and a glass of port-wine negus, for I am very hungry." And the King promptly brought them.

These were Frederic Hamilton's mother's links with the past. He himself could boast in 1924 that he had spoken to a survivor of Napoleon's calamitous Russian campaign:

"I was then seven years old and the old General de Flahault must have been seventy-eight or so, but it is curious that I should have heard from the actual lips of a man who had taken part in it, the account of the battle of Borodino, of the entry of the French troops into Moscow, of the burning of Moscow, and of the awful sufferings the French underwent during their disastrous retreat from Moscow. General de Flahault had been present at the terrible carnage of the crossing of the Beresina on 26 November, 1812, and had got both his feet frost-bitten there, whilst his faithful servant David had died from the effects of the cold. I wish that I could have been older then, or have had more historical knowledge, for it was a unique opportunity for acquiring information. I wish, too, that I could recall more of what M. de Flahault told me. I have quite vivid recollections of the old General himself, of the room in which we sat, and especially of the chocolates which formed so agreeable an accompaniment to our conversations. Still it remains an interesting link with the Napoleonic era. This is 1924; that was 1812!"

He also contrasted the difference in travel between the 1860's and the 1800's. His uncle Lord John Russell (later to be Prime Minister) took five days as a schoolboy in 1806 to make the journey between London and Dublin: three days by stagecoach to Holyhead, and thirty-eight hours crossing the Irish channel in a sailing-packet which got blown off-course so that the boy finally landed twenty-one miles from Dublin and had to take a post-chaise to reach home. The cost of this five-day jaunt was £31.16s., (£31·80p.) which to his nephew in 1924 seemed outrageous.

In 1860, in contrast, the railway and the steam-packet companies concerned had signed a contract with the Post Office, agreeing to convey the mails between London and Dublin in eleven hours – the railway and sea journey having up to then taken between fourteen and sixteen hours. It meant that the mail-trains had to cover the 264 miles between London and Holyhead at the unprecedented speed of 42 miles an hour, and people who trusted themselves to the *Wild Irishman* were thought very bold.

There was indeed a fearful accident, one of the worst of the century, on this very line in 1868, when Frederic, his mother, three sisters and two brothers, narrowly escaped being burnt to death. The Irish mail collided with a goods train laden with petroleum at Abergele in North Wales. Thirty-four people were killed, the lines were torn up, and the up-train from Holyhead was due any moment. There was nobody to give orders, as the engine driver had been killed, and the guard seriously injured, so Frederic's eldest brother took responsibility. He saw that the train was standing on a sharp slope, and at once uncoupled the undamaged carriages so that they could roll down the hill away from the burning wreckage. Then he ran at full-speed to the nearest signal-box a mile away, arriving just in time to get the up-train and all other traffic stopped.

"On his return my brother had a prolonged fainting fit, as the strain on his heart had been very great. It took the doctors over an hour to bring him round, and we all thought that he had died.

"I was eleven years old at the time, and the shock of the collision, the sight of the burning coaches, the screams of the women, the wreckage, and my brother's narrow escape from death, affected me for some little while afterwards."

Of London in the '60's Frederic Hamilton had depressing memories. It was, he said, very dark and dingy. Samuel Scott had remarked the same when he first saw it in 1851; he thought it shabby,

THE DISASTER AT ABERGELE

neglected and deafeningly noisy. Frederic wrote:

"The streets were sparingly lit with the dimmest of gas-jets set very far apart; the shop-windows made no display of lights, and the general effect was one of intense gloom. As most of the streets were still paved with granite blocks, the noise of London was far greater than at present. The whole air was full of a perpetual dull roar, to which one's ears grew so accustomed that when we left London for the country, the silence and stillness felt quite uncanny for the first two days."

But the young Hamiltons did not have to spend too much time in London. They had their own Irish home, Baron's Court, and English estates. And in 1866 for two years Dublin became their home. The nine-year-old Frederic came home from his first term at school to find that his father had been appointed Lord-Lieutenant of Ireland, and that they were in consequence to spend most of the year there.

One imagines that the appointment must have been quite popular in Ireland. Lord Abercorn was known as a kind ·and considerate landlord to his Irish tenants, and he championed the cause of Irish education, for which William Carleton would have blessed him. He was especially anxious that intermediate and university education should be available to Catholic children.

But naturally his youngest children gave no thought to this, nor did they seem particularly impressed by the dignity of having a father who was the Queen's own deputy in Ireland. They were far more concerned with what Dublin Castle and the Viceregal Lodge would be like to live in. They crossed from Holyhead in a special mail-steamer. (Years later Frederic was to hear that the four Dublin waiters who had been hired to serve the supper had been discovered dead drunk in the saloon, and had been thrust under the table, while the pantry boys were ordered to keep up a constant clatter of knives and forks to drown the noise of their snoring.) The ship had arrived too early for the State entry, and had cruised around outside the harbour to kill time. Unfortunately this made the ladies very sea-sick, and so the entry into Dublin to the accompaniment of booming guns, cheering and whistling must have been an ordeal. Frederic remembered all the flags and the streets lined with soldiers, and took it to be a tribute to him.

After Lord Abercorn had been sworn in at Dublin Castle, the family went off to the nearby Viceregal Lodge in Phoenix Park, for the Lord-Lieutenant had to spend only three months of the year in state at the Castle. The boys were by then very relieved to find that this was the case, and that they had not got to live perpetually surrounded by men in full uniform and by ladies in evening dresses as they thought from the morning's ceremonies they were fated to do.

They were never to be so fond of the Castle as they were of the Viceregal Lodge with its huge grounds, lake, woodlands, and private gate into the Zoological Gardens, but it did have its compensations. It would have been a wonderful place for playing if only there were not so many police, messengers, footmen and "a peculiarly officious breed of uniformed busybodies, who lived in little glass hutches, and pounced down upon little boys at unexpected moments with superfluous inquiries as to what they wanted there."

There was, for instance, the Privy Council Chamber. It had a huge centre table surrounded by benches, and three seats raised on a platform. Frederic and Ernest planned a splendid murder-trial if only they could get in, and they knew that their mother had a red cloak that could be used for the judge. But always the jack-in-office bobbed out from his glass cage and asked what they wanted.

Again, they had schemes for a tournament on the terrace, dressed

THE LORD MAYOR OF DUBLIN PRESENTING THE CITY KEYS TO THE NEW LORD LIEUTENANT

in the armour that hung on the Grand Staircase. But a policeman always foiled them when they tried to unhook it. They were forbidden to go into the State Rooms, and the Record Tower which had real medieval dungeons, was full of men diligently copying ancient manuscripts. And there was, said Frederic, a ridiculous fuss made when he was one day discovered behind the altar rails of the Chapel Royal, dressed in a surplice borrowed from the vestry, marrying his eight-year-old brother to a girl of the same age. "I had been so careful, too, to read the Marriage Service correctly."

Still, in spite of the endless prohibitions, there was plenty going on at the Castle. A band played daily in the Castle Yard; there was the daily mounting of the guard, and the schoolroom looked down on the infantry barrack-yard and the sound of bugle calls and rattling drums was the background to their life there. They also found a back way into the Throne Room, where they played at processions and investitures. They had seen their father conferring knighthoods, so they knew the procedure, and the sword of state and the mace were lying there in their red velvet cradles, ready to be used. "Should any of the staff of the present Governor-General care to examine the sword of state and the mace, they will find them both heavily dented. This is due to two small boys having frequently dropped them when they proved too heavy for their strength, during strictly private processions fifty-eight years ago."

The boys also discovered a little door near their bedroom which led directly into the gallery of St Patrick's Hall. Here the big dinners of from seventy to ninety people were held, and they used to creep in dressing gown and slippers to watch the scene in the brilliantly lit white and gold hall, the long tables blazing with plate and lights, the ladies in their jewels, the men in uniforms, while the edges of the hall had been transformed by thickets of greenhouse plants into a mock-equatorial forest in which coloured lamps gleamed.

"After the ladies had left, the uproar became deafening. In 1867 the old drinking habits had not yet died out, and though my father very seldom touched wine himself, he of course saw that his guests had sufficient; indeed, sufficient seems rather an elastic term, judging by what I saw and what I was told. Political, religious, and racial animosities had not yet assumed the intensely bitter character they have since reached in Ireland, and the traditional Irish wit, at present apparently dormant, still flashed, sparkled, and scintillated. From my hiding place in the gallery I could hear the roars of laughter the good stories provoked."

There were functions in which Frederic himself took part. Dressed in white satin breeches and lace ruffles he accompanied his father as a page on certain state occasions. He remembered the first "Drawing-Room" reception. It was the custom then for the Lord-Lieutenant to kiss every lady presented to him. At first Frederic thought the orgy of kissing was exceedingly funny, and wriggled with laughter. But as the evening wore on he became sleepier and sleepier, and suddenly looked up from where he was sitting on the steps of the throne to find that the powder from eight hundred cheeks and necks had turned his father's moustache and beard quite white.

In 1868 King Edward VII and Queen Alexandra (then of course Prince and Princess of Wales) came to Dublin Castle on an official visit, and the whole stay was an unending round of festivities. The Princess was a most beautiful woman, and Frederic adored her – so

much that when his father alluded to her at some great public ceremony as "the lovely and gracious lady who honours us today with her
presence by my side", Frederic, all tricked out in his page's uniform
by his father's side, burst into shrill cheers.

For the ceremonies of this visit, the numbers of the pages had been
increased to five, and these included Frederic's eleven-year-old
nephew, Charles Lambton. They were given splendid new uniforms
with gold-embroidered white satin waistcoats, but they thought little
of these; it was the swords with real steel blades that enchanted them,
and the ten-year-old uncle and the eleven-year-old nephew decided
that they must have a duel in the garden. They had just reached a
secluded place and were making thrusts at each other when the
grown-ups fell upon them and carried them off in disgrace. After
that pages' swords were fitted with wooden blades only.

The last and most elaborate ceremony of all was the installation of
the Prince of Wales as a Knight of St Patrick in St Patrick's Cathedral.

"The pages were constantly being drilled in the Cathedral, in
order to perfect us in our parts, for the ceremonial was very elaborate.
We had, all five of us, amongst other things, to walk backwards down
some steps, keeping in line and keeping step. For five small boys to
do this neatly without awkwardness, requires a great deal of practice.

"The procession to the Cathedral was made in full state, the streets
being lined with troops, and the carriages, with their escorts of
cavalry, going at a foot's pace through the principal thoroughfares
of Dublin. I remember it chiefly on account of the bitter north-east
wind blowing. The five pages drove together in an open carriage,
and received quite an ovation from the crowd, but nobody had
thought of providing them with overcoats. Silk stockings, satin knee-
breeches and lace ruffles are very inadequate protection against an
Arctic blast, and we arrived at the Cathedral stiff and torpid with
cold.

"The ceremony was very gorgeous and imposing, and as the pages
were all the while in attendance on the two principal persons concerned, we got an admirable view of it. My father as Grand Master
of the Order invested the Prince and gave him the accolade, after
which he and the Archbishop of Dublin placed the new Knight in
his proper stall amidst a great blare of trumpets. I remember being
immensely impressed when the procession of Knights of St Patrick
swept in from the Lady-Chapel in their flowing sky-blue satin

mantles, and Sir Bernard Burke, the Ulster King-of-Arms, filled me
with joy, for in his heraldic tabard he looked exactly like the King in
a pack of cards. I was reading *Alice in Wonderland** at the time, and
when "Ulster" attended by two heralds, all three of them in tabards,
advanced to the Choir steps to proclaim amidst further fanfares of
trumpets, the new Knight's "title and style", I thought that I had
tumbled straight into the trial scene, for they looked for all the world
like the King and Knave of Hearts and the Knave of Diamonds."

Frederic Hamilton might have felt in 1924 that the political
atmosphere in Ireland was more bitter than in his father's time, but
in the 1860's there was violence in the air. The Ribbonmen of
William Carleton's time had been succeeded by an even more
menacing Irish nationalist movement, the Fenians, whose activities
did not just limit themselves to Ireland. There were Fenians in the
United States who, in their efforts to overthrow British rule in
Ireland, attempted an invasion of Canada. There were Fenian bomb
outrages in England, including a plot to blow up Clerkenwell

* Published in 1865, it would still have been a novelty.

prison. And in Dublin itself, Frederic, Ernest and their sister, recovering from measles, found themselves in the middle of the Fenian rising of 1867, though to them it was all an exciting game.

"We were already convalescent, when one evening a mysterious stranger arrived from the Castle [they had been sent to the Viceregal Lodge to avoid spreading infection] and had an interview with the governess. As a result of that interview the kindly old lady began clucking like a scared hen, fussed quite prodigiously, and told us to collect our things at once as we were to start for the Castle in a quarter of an hour. After a frantically hurried packing, we were bustled into the carriages, the mysterious stranger taking his seat on the box. To our surprise we saw some thirty mounted Hussars at the door. As we moved off, to our unspeakable delight, the Hussars drew their swords and closed in on the carriage, one riding at either window. And so we drove through Dublin. We had never had an escort before, and felt immensely elated and dignified. At the Castle there seemed to be some confusion. I heard doors banging and people moving about all through the night.

"Long afterwards I learnt that the great Fenian rising was fixed for that night. The authorities had heard that part of the Fenian plan was to capture the Viceregal Lodge and to hold the Lord Lieutenant's children as hostages, which explains the arrival at the Lodge of Chief Inspector Dunn, the frantic haste, and the escort of Hussars with drawn swords.

"That night an engagement, or it might more justly be termed a skirmish, did take place between the Fenians and the troops at Tallagh, some twenty miles from Dublin. My brothers and most of my father's staff had been present, which explained the mysterious noises during the night.

"As a result of this fight, some three hundred prisoners were taken, and Lord Strathnairn, then Commander-in-Chief in Ireland, was very hard put to it to find sufficient men to escort the prisoners into Dublin. Lord Strathnairn suddenly got an inspiration. He had every single button, brace buttons and all, cut off the prisoners' trousers. Then the men had perforce, for decency's sake, to hold their trousers together with their hands, and I defy anyone similarly situated to run more than a yard or two.

"The prisoners were all paraded in the Castle yard next day, and I walked out among them. As they had been up all night in very heavy

THE FENIAN INSURRECTION: CONFLICT WITH THE POLICE, UNDER SUB-INSPECTOR BURKE, AT TALLAGHT, NEAR DUBLIN.

rain, they all looked very forlorn and miserable. The Castle gates were shut that day, for the first time in the memory of the oldest inhabitant, and they remained shut for four days.

"Dublin was seething with unrest, so on that very afternoon my father and mother drove very slowly, quite alone, without an Aide-de-Camp or escort, in a carriage-and-four with outriders, through all the poorest quarters in Dublin. They were well received, and there was no hostile demonstration whatever. The idea of the slow drive through the slums was my mother's. She wished to show that though the Castle gates were closed, she and my father were not afraid. I saw her on her return when she was looking very pale and drawn, but I was too young to realize what the strain must have been. My mother's courage was loudly praised, but I think that my friends O'Connor and little Byrne, the postilions, also deserve quite a good mark, for they ran the same amount of risk, and they were not entirely free agents in the matter as my father and mother were."

In 1868 there was a change of government and a new Lord-Lieutenant was appointed. Frederic's father, by then the Duke of Abercorn, returned to Dublin in 1874 for a further two years, but by that time all his family was grown-up and there was nobody to play pirates on the lake of the Viceregal Lodge or hunt Red Indians in its woodlands, or try to steal the armour at the Castle.

NOBILITY GOING TO THE DRAWING-ROOM.

Molly

THE MODERN GIRL

BEFORE 1880 nobody seemed to think that girls changed very much from one generation to the next. And then suddenly the words "the modern girl" appear. *Punch* made jokes about her; magazines for ladies talked brightly of her; articles in the *Girl's Realm* and the *Girl's Own Paper* solemnly discussed the duties and the aspirations of "the girl of the period".

When Molly Thomas went down to Cornwall in 1887 to see her favourite aunt, she asked eagerly about her cousins. Her aunt was cautious.

"'I think they are rather dreading you as a 'modern girl.'

'What a funny idea! What is a modern girl, Tony?'

'Well, you have been to a big modern school, and to Cambridge, and they think you know a lot, and may ride the high horse – absurd idea of course.'"

The "modern girl", according to the same Molly, also was likely to ride a bicycle, travel on the top of a bus, and go in for mixed bathing. This new female was strong-minded and independent, and it was her education that was responsible for this. Very likely she went to one of the large new day schools, where, besides learning subjects which only boys had been taught before, she mixed with a far wider range of social classes than the girl who had been brought up at home or sent to a small school for young ladies.

For centuries girls' education had varied very little. Either they had been taught at home, by their parents, an elder sister, or a governess, or perhaps they had gone to an establishment where thirty pupils would have been thought a large number.

Elizabeth Grant and her sisters learned with a governess whom they hated – though probably less than Miss Elphick hated them: wild Highland children who did not hesitate to show her how much they despised her, "an illiterate woman of very ungovernable temper, whose ideas had been gathered from a class lower than we could possibly have been acquainted with, and whose habits were those of a servant."

But the Grants had to rub along with Miss Elphick as best they could. It would have been difficult to bring anybody else to the remote valley in the Highlands, even if somebody better could be found. "We learned the harp, pianoforte and singing after a fashion," said Elizabeth, "drawing in several styles, geography with map-making well taught, and arithemetic very well taught, more knowledge of the stars than I cared for; lists of stars and maps of the sky . . . We had chronological tables to make which delighted me, pieces of poetry to learn by heart, and French translations and exercises." They played to their father, and listened to him as he read from books, reviews and newspapers. If it had not been for Miss Elphick, Elizabeth might have enjoyed learning, though practising the harp for an hour before breakfast throughout bitter Highland winters, in a pitch dark, unheated drawing-room (you did not need a candle to play scales) would always bring her near to tears.

The Bothams did not employ a governess; this would have been thought very pretentious in the small town of Uttoxeter. Mrs Botham taught Mary and Anna herself until, as we have seen, they were sent to school in the far-distant south of England.* This

* In the year that the Bothams went to school – 1809 – the term "schoolgirl" first entered the English language, according to the Oxford English Dictionary.

The School Girl in 1820 by W. Upton

SHEWING THE SAMPLER.

THE colour'd Sampler's work displays
The stitch and mark in various ways,
For ev'ry observer's tongue to praise
THE SCHOOL-GIRL!

THE GENERAL EXAMINATION.

RELATIONS, friends, now that, now this,
Flock round t'give th'heart-glad kiss
And hail with rapturous innate bliss
THE SHOOL-GIRL!

GOING TO SCHOOL.

THE darling Child sweet Pledge of Love!
Playful, and innocent as the dove,
With fine new shoes, sets out to prove
THE SCHOOL-GIRL!

THE SCHOOL.

HOW fast she learns! how neat she sews!
How soon each task she gets and knows!
The watchful Governess proudly shews
THE SCHOOL-GIRL!

NEEDLE WORK.

EMBROID'RY, flowers, and Plain work too
Th'docile maiden shews to view;
In ev'ry branch a scholar true
THE SCHOOL-GIRL!

THE DANCING MASTER.

THE graceful Dance next wins the Child,
(Sweet emblem of Affection mild.)
In manners pure, in spirits wild
THE SCHOOL-GIRL!

TEACHING GEOGRAPHY.

GEOGRAPHY'S instructive Page,
The product of ev'ry clime and age,
Unfolds its volume t'engage
THE SCHOOL-GIRL!

HOLIDAYS.

THE sportive Holidays, clad in smiles,
That many a care fraught hour beguiles,
Re welcome home with harmless wiles
THE SCHOOL-GIRL!

school in Croydon was typical of many such establishments of its day: ten or twelve pupils with a head governess, and two assistants hardly older than the senior girls.

Lessons played a very small part in Mary's memories of the place. She recalled how they each had a garden of their own, and how they went for long summer expeditions through the Surrey countryside, led by a teacher, and with a servant at the back of the procession wheeling "a light tilted wagon containing abundant provisions for our midday meal."

The other girls, Mary remembered, did fancy work while the Bothams stitched shirts for their father. "We had never learnt to net, nor had we ever seen before fine strips of coloured paper plaited into delicate patterns, or split straw worked into a pattern in coarse net." Their school life only lasted two years, and then they went home. "Thomas Goodall, the master of the only boys' school in the town, was engaged to teach us spelling, Latin, the globes, and indeed whatever else he could impart." And Mary and Anna were set to teach their little brother and sister, and some poor children to whom they gave lessons twice a week in the stable loft.

It was to correct this haphazard sort of education that Frances Mary Buss in 1850 began the school that was to become the North London Collegiate School – the school that Molly Thomas entered in 1883 at the advanced age of sixteen, from a private school where she had been very happy, though most of what she had learnt had been picked up from her mother or her brothers.

By 1883 there were many other girls' High Schools in existence; women could now become graduates of London University and study at Girton and Newnham Colleges in Cambridge (though the university there would not award them degrees). The modern girl had arrived.

The *Girl's Own Paper* was one of those that gave much thought to this new species. It catered for girls from thirteen to twenty-five, and it took care to point out to "modern girls" that home duties were the most important duties of all. So, though there were competitions for essays, there were also ones for plain sewing (the judges usually complained that the standard of the entries was disgracefully low), and there was more about fancy work and cooking than about bookish subjects. And though there was an article about Miss Buss and the North London Collegiate School, there was also an article by a clergyman's daughter on "The Disadvantages of Higher

THE PRINCESS OF WALES PRESENTING PRIZES AT THE NORTH LONDON COLLEGIATE SCHOOL FOR GIRLS.

Education". (This very much annoyed a fourteen-year-old named Bertha Jenkinson who told the editor that "if God had intended woman to be merely man's slave he would never have furnished her with reasoning power.")

The article about Miss Buss's school appeared in 1882, the year before Molly Thomas went there, and this writer, at any rate, seemed very clear that higher education for girls had come to stay. She described the buildings, which had been opened in 1879 by the Prince and Princess of Wales, and was especially impressed by the examination hall of oak and red brick, "the munificent gift of the Clothworkers' Company." She admired the classrooms where the desks of shortsighted pupils were raised specially high to bring the books nearer their eyes. The cloakrooms had hot pipes to dry wet

220

clothes. There was a gymnasium "furnished with parallel and horizontal bars, ropes and ladders, dumb bells, etc.," a chemical laboratory, and a lecture theatre where Miss Buss gave "little addresses on subjects relative to the moral life and well being of the school." There was also a sewing room and a drawing school.

"School begins at 9.15, the school doors being opened at 9, and any stranger walking about that time up the Camden or Sandall-roads must be literally amazed at the streams of girls pouring into these roads from all quarters, and flowing steadily in one direction. Indeed, it is not often that one has the opportunity of seeing so many girls together, for the school numbers 490 pupils."

The school curriculum consisted of Scripture, mathematics, arithmetic, natural science, Latin, French and German, history, English language and literature, geography, drawing, economics, and class singing. Greek was taught to those going to London University, and there was sewing and music in the afternoons, though no formal lessons were given after 1.30. "Mathematics are taught as low down as the Fourth Form. This branch of study is entered into by the pupils with a spirit that would certainly be a source of extreme surprise, if not of dissatisfaction, to those who still continue to pronounce the studies of geometry and algebra 'quite unsuited to the female mind.'"

Discipline, said the writer, was enforced by a healthy public opinion. There were form monitors, and there were school prefects, while small breaches of rules had to be entered by the girl herself in the Appearing Book. Too many appearances in the book meant that the girl was summoned to Miss Buss.

No doubt the writer remembered that a great many parents in the '80's were alarmed at the thought of having a daughter turned by school into "a girl of the period", so she finished by assuring her readers how very womanly and gracious Miss Buss and her teachers were: "Many a parent, whose daughters have been educated by Miss Buss, is only too proud to acknowledge that, in coming into contact with a lady of such high intellectual power, such real refine-ment and true tenderness, his children have gained a conception of the possible dignity of womanhood, which is of even more value to them than the excellent instruction given in the school."

Molly Thomas was not so uncritical. She thought that the education Miss Buss provided was a feeble imitation of boys' schools, with far too much emphasis on the passing of exams, and that the minimum of useful things were taught with the maximum of fuss.

But she had been wildly enthusiastic to go there. Her mother on her sixteenth birthday had given her a choice; did she want to be a lady of leisure or be independent and earn her living. Molly was quite certain that she wanted to be independent, but how?

"In those days it was not considered the thing for a girl to 'earn', although she might toy with a little work. Any other career than teaching was practically unknown. During my last term at [my private] school one of the girls had told me that a friend of hers knew a girl who had actually become a B.A. We had both been awe-struck that a woman one might meet could attain such glory, but we neither of us connected this pinnacle with an ordinary teacher in a school. Indeed, I fancied that one just 'took up' teaching in the same casual way that I had taken a Sunday-school class last summer in Cornwall."

Clearly she needed more learning than her little private school had provided, and when her Cornish aunt had offered to pay her fees, she knew at once where she wanted to go – to Miss Buss's North London Collegiate School, "the biggest school in England and the finest," as an acquaintance had bragged to her; where the Princess of Wales herself gave away the prizes.

She was rather dashed by the entrance exam, it was "so pifflingly easy", all except the buttonhole which she had no idea how to make until her mother showed her. She then had to make a second journey to the school to stitch it, for it was a rule that no girl could enter who couldn't make a buttonhole. She was even more dashed when she had her first lesson with the Upper Fourth.

"After my dreams of cultured teachers and keen-brained girls – how humiliating was the drop! An empty desk among some thirty others was pointed out to me with a hurried 'Sit there, dear.' Something that seemed like geography was in progress, and the girls were being questioned round out of Cornwell's Geography, a text-book only too familiar to me. After an astonished taking in of the dreadful reality I relieved my feelings by a contemptuous remark to the girl in the adjoining desk. She placed a warning finger on her mouth, but was too late. The teacher had heard an unwarranted voice and

beckoned me to her desk. Thrusting an open exercise-book towards me she said,

'You must sign, dear.'

'Sign? Sign what?' I asked in bewilderment.

'Write down "I spoke in geography" and sign your name, dear,' she replied, hurriedly resuming a question on the Welland canal."

Molly, in fact, was a "modern girl" before she ever arrived at the North London Collegiate School. Her brothers had encouraged her to mock at old-maidish fussings at school; she was independent, forthright, and she had already ridden on top of a bus before she was eleven. Miss Buss's school might give girls the sort of systematic education that only boys had had before, but it set out to train them along old-fashioned lines, and independence was certainly not encouraged.

It was the rules that Molly found so depressing. Each new girl was presented with a list of them in small print and in double columns.

In addition new ones appeared almost every day, like "Broken needles must not be thrown on the floor." They were forbidden to get wet on the way to school, to walk more than three in a row, to drop a pencil-box, hang a boot-bag by only one loop, to answer before they were asked in class. If a girl happened to fall over a blackboard Molly was sure that there would be a rule against that on the noticeboard next day. Every time à rule was broken it had to be entered in the Appearing Book. "You'll have to sign for that, dear," a voice called out from a distant cloakroom when Molly dropped a pencil box and thanked her stars that nobody was there to see. Girls with more tender consciences would have signed the book unprompted; many of them tormented themselves with wondering whether they ought to sign if they jostled another girl and so far forgot themselves as to apologize – for talking was the worst of all the crimes.

Too many appearances in the Appearing Book meant that you were called before Miss Buss. Even the strongest quailed at the thought of that. She harangued mercilessly until her victim burst into tears, then she was dismissed, the storm was over. But it was a searing experience. Molly remembered how one day the English mistress stood up her class without warning and marched them, to their incredulous horror, to Miss Buss's sanctum. She was not there, but obviously she was on her way to them.

Unnerved, they stood there in silence wondering what storm was going to break over their heads this time. Then from the door came the sharp order, "Turn. Pass out. Go back to your form room." And they returned to the English lesson as though nothing had happened. Nor were they particularly surprised by the episode; they accepted it as just another of the meaningless orders that were given to you at school, like dogs were commanded to beg or lie down. It was a few days later that they found out the point, when they were told at their next English lesson to write an essay on what they had observed in the room. Only one girl managed to put anything down, Bessie Jones who always had a clear conscience. The others had been far too agitated to notice their surroundings.

Rules, and dreary teaching by what Molly scornfully described as "the textbook and water method" made that first term very miserable. There was all the fussing about marks, too; endless time was taken up by counting them, entering them in huge books, adding them and checking them. They were the life-blood of the school, and to be certain that nobody acquired a mark to which she was not entitled the desks were fitted with iron sockets so that boards could be slotted in during tests as a screen between one girl's work and the next. Even the evenings were not your own, because there were rigid rules about how long girls should take over their homework and every minute spent had to be laboriously counted and added up and a parent's signature obtained.

The terrifying Miss Buss was one of the least of Molly's worries, for she had discovered early that Miss Buss liked the forthright girls who stood up to her. On Molly's first day at the school, when she was wandering helplessly down corridors from which every girl had vanished, looking despairingly for the Upper Fourth form room, she ran into a little white-haired old woman whom she took to be a cleaner, and asked her casually for help. The cleaner turned out to be Miss Buss, not at all pleased by Molly's manner. But Molly, instead of being daunted, said cheerfully: "Oh, then *you* are sure to know the way to the Upper Fourth, and I do so want to know."

Later on, when she was in the Sixth Form, she discovered that Miss Buss was warm-hearted, generous and impulsive, given to hugging her favourites. The girls, sometimes even the teachers, recognizing Molly to be one of these, expected her to be their spokeswoman on awkward occasions. But even Molly sometimes did not dare. There was a point with Miss Buss beyond which the boldest could not go – like the time when she gave the Sixth Form the same lecture on humour two weeks running. The first time it was very funny, full of gay reminiscences and good jokes, and the girls rose to it with spirit, laughing hugely, much to Miss Buss's gratification. The second time was a different matter. Miss Buss, apparently quite unconscious that she was repeating herself, paused in the same places waiting for laughter, but none came. Nobody could bring herself to interrupt the lecture and explain, though the girls and the form mistress gave Molly sidelong beseeching glances. "That was all very well, but there were limits even to my audacity." When at the end Miss Buss did have the matter explained to her, outside the form room, her anger was terrible. "'Why didn't you stop me? Why didn't *you*, Mary?'" she kept saying accusingly to poor Molly.

Such scolding, however, was the exception in the Sixth. The rules, the niggling about marks, seemed a cloud which might hang over the rest of the school but not over them. The teaching was good, too. Instead of wretchedly-educated women sitting with Latin cribs on their laps, pretending that they knew the language, they had a classics mistress who really knew her subject and knew how to teach. They were encouraged to help each other; lessons were discussions to which they all contributed; Miss Buss consulted the prefects among them about the running of the school. Molly settled down to enjoy this new intellectual freedom. Up till now she had thought a little wistfully of her old private school and its casual ways and liberal playtime.

But in the Sixth you did begin to wonder about your future. In the 1880's it was hardly a question of what career; rather, you had to decide whether you wanted to teach with this new learning you had acquired, or retreat into your home until you were sought in marriage. Miss Buss put the matter squarely to Molly's brother, Tom, who had been summoned to the school to give advice about the staging of a play.

" 'You young men have an easy time . . . Now that sister of yours, if I don't rescue her, is destined to the dreadful career of stopping at home and helping mother – dusting the drawing-room, arranging the flowers, and other horrors.'

'I know,' said Tom, 'and mother and all of us want her to do something better, and you can't think how grateful we all are to you for all . . .'

'Yes, yes,' she interrupted. 'Now what I say is, Why did the Lord create Messrs. Huntley and Palmer to make cakes for us, if not to give our clever girls a chance to do something better?' "

The something better that she chose for Molly was a chance to go to a newly-founded teachers' training college in Cambridge. It was an entirely new venture. Until then nobody had been taught how to teach; the men were university graduates, the women, if they were lucky, had been to a school like the North London Collegiate and then were pitchforked into a classroom, most of them only semi-literate like many of the staff even there.

Miss Buss and other enthusiasts were hard at work trying to raise teaching into a real profession, like law or medicine. " 'Here we are,' they were saying, 'with a big school and a deplorable deficiency of really good teachers. Let us pick a few of our best girls and venture some money in training them properly for their job.' Of course I

(Drawn by Madena Moore.)

SWEET GIRL GRADUATES.

knew nothing at the time of all this activity behind the scenes. The first news of it that reached me was that I had been selected as one of the four North Londoners who were to be among the first students in 'a new college at Cambridge.'"

And so equipped with three "new" dresses (one for every day, one for dinner, and one for Sundays) passed on to her by a young and fashionable aunt, Molly made the transition between girlhood to young ladyhood, from London to Cambridge. The dresses "took ages to get into, with their close-fitting bodices, endless hooks and buttons, skirts to the ankle, and a kind of gathering-up behind called a crinolette. But they fitted all right when once on, and the pleasure of looking grown-up atoned for my diminished mobility."

Her mother packed her trunk with everything she could think of, on the model of the White Knight, and stood waving off the cab that was taking Molly to Liverpool Street Station and thence to Cambridge. And in Cambridge she was to find herself called Miss Thomas and the occupant of a room of her own to sit in – even to lock and label "engaged". She was grown-up, and she was independent.

Ernest and Flora

JUBILATION DAY

"ANOTHER day is over now," wrote Mary Howitt on 20 June, 1887, "that the longest and our Queen's Jubilee. I wonder how they have gone on in London and all over England. Our Union Jack is up and makes a great show. I rose in good time and went to Mass in the parish-church." She was in Germany then, an old lady, nearing ninety, one of the few of those left who could remember the last Golden Jubilee in 1809.

In 1957 Ernest Shepard wrote down his memories of the Queen's Jubilee. He was seven years old in 1887, living in St John's Wood, two or three miles north of that part of London where most of the celebration was going on, but very much aware of it all the same. He and his brother Cyril had picked up a song from the local tradesboys, and sang it all over the house.

Hooray! Hooray! for Jubilation Day!
'Tis only once in fifty years, so people say.
We all got mixed and had a jolly spree,
A'going with the missus to the Jubilee!

"We all got tight" was the original version, but Martha the maid told them that this was not a very nice thing to say, and even if their parents did not mind, their aunts might. Ernest would have had no idea that his Jubilee was not unique. When you are seven you live in the present. He was vaguely aware that there had been other kings on the throne, for the gas-lamps near his home had $\boxed{\begin{array}{c} \text{IV} \\ \hline \text{G.R.} \end{array}}$ on them which Martha told the children meant a king.

From early summer the excitement grew intense, and London was decking itself for the great event. There were flags, and V.R. signs with fairy lights. The linen draper's window was a riot of flags of all nations, there were small Union Jacks at 4½d. each, (2p.) and larger ones of many countries at 1s. 1½d. (5½p.). Ernest had saved 2s. 7d., (13p.) so, while his brother and sister, Cyril and Ethel, bought little Union Jacks, he settled for a large red, yellow and black flag, and 2½d. (1p.) worth of red ribbons to make a bow for Septimus, the adored toy horse on wheels that he trundled up and down the pavement outside the house. But the flag turned out to be a Belgian one, and his father thought that it ought not to be displayed so conspicuously as the Union Jacks.

"We heard wonderful tales of the decorations being put up in the main streets. Martha had been to see them, and we were delighted when Mother said she would take us to Oxford street to see them for ourselves. We went after lunch, boarding an 'Atlas' bus at the corner of the Terrace. Cyril and I were allowed to clamber up the steep steps, helped by the conductor, and were then handed along by the passengers, who sat back to back on the long middle seat. There was no railing to prevent one falling off, only a low board, so we clung tightly as we were handed forward. I was first, and in consequence secured a place on the box seat beside the driver, where a man made room for me and fixed the tarpaulin apron.

"A woman was never seen on top of a bus, the climb up was too steep for the long skirts of the times, though a young friend of Mother's called Poppy once clambered up to the consternation of the inside passengers."

The ride to Oxford Circus was full of excitement; there was an atmosphere of important bustle everywhere: slowly moving crowds of sightseers, a babel of voices, the sound of hammering as workmen fixed boards in front of the shops. There were garlands of paper flowers, a triumphal archway across the top of Regent street inscribed 'VICTORIA! ALL NATIONS SALUTE YOU!', and down the street a vista of notices hung from house to house saying 'EMPIRE, JUBILEE, BRITISH ISLES.' There were stands erected in front of many of the shops, covered in yellow-fringed red baize, and wire crowns with V.R. signs which would be later hung with fairy lamps.

Soldiers came along, and to the excitement of the crowds they stopped in Oxford Circus and were formed up in line while an officer paced out distances. A man selling flags told the children that they were rehearsing for lining the route of the procession. The children were hot and tired by this time, and delighted when their mother said that they could have tea at a confectioner's, and still more delighted when ices were ordered.

Jubilee Day dawned grey and misty, the sort of greyness that turns to a brilliantly hot day. They were all up early, because the parents were going to see the processional drive from a stand on the route and had to be in their seats long before it began. Martha was going to take the children to Regent's Park to see the parade of the Boys' Brigade and of the school children. They admired their mother in her striped blue and white dress, flowered bonnet, and tiny parasol, and were rather overcome by the grandeur of their father in frock coat and top hat.

There were huge crowds in Regent's Park to see the processions there, and Martha even had to ask a policeman for help to take the small party to the park gates. It was a Reserve policeman, as the others were all down controlling the crowds on the main procession route.

"Presently the procession came in sight, led by the bands of the Boys' Brigade. The drum-major, wearing a sort of busby with a plume, was a wonderful sight. He had gauntlet gloves and a sash across his chest, and flourished a staff, throwing it around like a juggler. Some of the bandsmen were very young, but all were blowing away lustily and I was filled with envy of the drummers, the big drummer particularly, for he had a leopard-skin that nearly reached the

CITY OF CHICHESTER

THE QUEEN'S JUBILEE

The Jubilee will be celebrated in the City on

Tuesday, June 21, 1887.

PROGRAMME.

Citizens are invited to **DECORATE THEIR PREMISES** with
Flags, Flowers, Bunting, &c., &c., and
TO ILLUMINATE THEIR HOUSES AT NIGHT.

AT 8 A.M. there will be a Royal Salute of 21 Aerial Maroons.

At 8.45 A.M. THE MAYOR AND CORPORATION will assemble in the
COUNCIL CHAMBER, and proceed to the RECREATION GROUND.
Robed.

AT 9 A.M. the Mayor will Plant a Tree there, in commemoration of the
Jubilee.

There will also assemble in the Recreation Ground, at the same time, to
witness the Ceremony and to form

A PROCESSION

To MORNING SERVICE in the CATHEDRAL, at 10.30 a.m., in the
subjoined order :

The Band of the Royal Sussex L. I. Militia.
The Mace.
The Mayor and Corporation.
The Magistrates.
The Board of Guardians.
The Rifle Volunteers in Uniform.
The Members of the Jubilee Committee.
The Fire Brigade in Uniform.

The **Members** of the Friendly Societies in the City, arranged according to their date of formation, with
their Flags, Banners, and Insignia :

1.—The Loyal "Rock" Lodge of the Manchester Unity of Independent Order of Odd Fellows.
2.—The Good Intent Benefit Society.
3.—The Court "Constantia" of the Ancient Order of Foresters Friendly Society.
4.—The Court "Prince of Wales" ditto.
5.—The Loyal "Perseverance" Lodge of the Manchester Unity of Independent Order of Odd Fellows.
6.—The "Angel" Provident Society.

The Boys of the Whitby School.

The **Procession** will march up East Street, down North Street, round the North Walls, up West Street,
and Down South Street to Canon Gate, where it will meet

AT 10.15, THE DEAN AND CHAPTER

And the PAROCHIAL CLERGY, who, with the CITY CHOIRS, will precede the Procession along
Canon Lane and up S. Richard's Walk, into the Cathedral by the West Door.

Immediately after the Service, the CORPORATION will take **LUNCHEON**
with the **MAYOR** in the COUNCIL CHAMBER.

A DINNER WILL BE GIVEN TO 1000 CITIZENS

800 will dine in the Corn Exchange & 200 at their own homes.

The Band of the Royal Sussex Regiment will play in the Exchange during Dinner.

AT **1.30** 1,800 CHILDREN will assemble in the CATTLE MARKET, where they will be PHOTOGRAPHED by Mr. W. N. Malby, who will subsequently present each child with a copy.

AT **2.30** the Children will march in Procession up the East Street and down the North Street to

THE PRIORY PARK,

Where they will be entertained with Exhibitions of Punch and Judy, and Marionettes, Races, and Children's Games.

The Band of the Royal Sussex L. I. Militia will accompany the Procession.

During the Afternoon the BAND of the ROYAL SUSSEX REGIMENT will play in the Park.

The CHILDREN WILL HAVE TEA AT **4.30** *P.M.*, and each child will be given a " Jubilee Mug."

AT **3** there will be

SPORTS IN THE RECREATION GROUND,

Consisting of a Donkey Race, a Donkey Steeplechase, an Obstacle Race, a Race by Veterans, other Races, Climbing the Greasy Pole, Jumping in Sacks, Tug of War, &c., &c.

The BAND of the ROYAL SUSSEX L. I. MILITIA will play in the RECREATION GROUND during the Afternoon.

AT **9.30** *P.M.*

THE CITY WILL BE ILLUMINATED WITH ELECTRICITY

With JAPANESE LANTERNS, and with GAS, and other designs, the principal features of which will be :

Four Arc Electric Lights around the Cross.	Another Arc Electric Light in the East Street.
Festoons of Electric Glow Lamps underneath the Cross.	An Arc Electric Light in the West Street.
An Arc Electric Light at the Mayor's Residence.	An Arc Electric Light in the South Street.
An Arc Electric Light at the Town Clerk's Residence.	And a Gas Design on the Council Chamber.

AT 9 *P.M.*

A TORCHLIGHT PROCESSION,

Accompanied by the BAND of the ROYAL SUSSEX L. I. MILITIA, will form in the Cattle Market, and march along the Cattle Market Road and South Street to the Railway Gates, returning up South Street, down West Street, through Orchard Street and Orchard Terrace, up the Old Broyle Road, along High Street, down the New Broyle Road, up North Street, down East Street, along Saint Pancras, to the Recreation Ground.

AT **10** *P.M.* there will be

A GRAND DISPLAY OF FIREWORKS

In the RECREATION GROUND, with Fire Balloons, Coloured Lights, &c., &c.

The Band of the Royal Sussex Regiment will play during the Exhibition.

DECORATED ARCHES WILL BE ERECTED ON THE SITES OF THE ANCIENT GATES OF THE CITY.

£1,100

Will be subsequently expended in improving the PUBLIC ELEMENTARY SCHOOLS in the City.

God Save the Queen.

WM. SMITH, *Mayor*.

Chichester, 1st June, 1887.

WILMSHURST, PRINTER, CHICHESTER.

ground. What fun it would be, I thought, to have a big drum and bang it along the Terrace!

"When the procession had passed the crowd began to break up, drifting into the Park to sit on the grass and refresh themselves. It was so hot that we were glad to get back home and have some cool lemonade and then lie down. Father had promised to take us out in the evening to see the illuminations.

"Before I lay down, I went to the top drawer in the yellow chest and took out my copybook, the one I always drew special things in, and with the pencil Mother had given me from a dance programme I tried to draw some of the events of the day. Somehow, nothing could come right, the pencil would not work, suck it as I might.

"I was nearly asleep when I heard the sound of horses. It wasn't just cabs or buses. It was something much more exciting. Tumbling out of bed, I ran to the window in time to see Her Majesty's Royal Horse Artillery, busbies, shell jackets, yellow braid and all, with an officer resplendent in his blue and yellow uniform riding in front. Behind him on a white horse, rode a very young trumpeter. Then came the guns, rattling along. I had often seen the gunners exercising their horses, but never, never had I seen them in all their glory. I knew they were on their way back to barracks.

"It seemed a long time after tea before it got dark enough and we were allowed to start lighting our illuminations. The fairy lights in coloured glass shades had to be fitted with nightlights and carried out to put along the balcony outside the drawing room. I insisted on lighting one of these, and made a mess of it, scorching my fingers and dropping the taper inside the glass where it sputtered. Then I had no better luck with the Chinese lantern, which I have since found is always difficult to light. This time I set fire to the paper, and the whole thing went flaming into the area below. Further attempts were then stopped by Father. When all the illuminations had been lit we trooped down and out of the front door to see the effect. It was not so good as the house three doors away, but still it was very gay.

"Cyril and I were jumping up and down in our eagerness to get started, but first we had to sit down and eat some sandwiches and drink a glass of milk.

"There was a glow in the sky, and Park Road, usually rather gloomy after dark, with only a few gas lamps, was now a blaze of light. People were out in the street or else gossiping by their front doors. Coles the linen drapers had a beautiful star sign in flickering

MESSRS. PEARS' ILLUMINATIONS, OXFORD-STREET.

gas with V.R. at each side. Most of the windows had fairy lights along the window sills. The little dressmaker's shop near Clarence Gate had rows of candles in the windows and Maltby the tailor was particularly grand. But it was only when the bus landed us near Oxford Circus that the full glory burst upon us.

235

"Almost every shop had some sign lighted up with lamps or gas, and a number of people in the crowd were carrying lighted Chinese lanterns. Men and women in little groups were dancing together to the music of concertinas, and gangs of youths were making nuisances of themselves by parading in long caterpillars and pushing their way, swinging and shouting, through the throng. There was no traffic in Oxford street, which was just as well, for it could not have moved; the whole roadway was packed with people pushing slowly along one way or the other, or coming to a stop in front of some particularly showy display.

"It wasn't long before I, with my little legs, felt quite stifled down among the skirts of the crowd. I was lifted up on Father's shoulders, where I could get a splendid view of everything, but, what with the day's excitements and all, I began to feel very sleepy, and to nod. Mother saw this and said, 'Harry, I think it is time we went home.' No voice was raised in protest, and we began to fight our way out of the press. It took a long time to get clear and longer still to find a four-wheeler. Once safely inside, Cyril and I promptly fell asleep, and I was carried up to bed with the sounds of London celebrating getting ever fainter in my ears."

Down in Oxfordshire they had also been celebrating. Flora Timms who lived in a tiny hamlet that she called "Lark Rise" in her memories of late Victorian rural life, though its real name is Juniper Hill, went with everybody else in the parish to the park of a local landowner. Three villages were joining for tea and sports and dancing and fireworks. Nothing like it had been known there before.

Even in Juniper with its few cottages clustered round a furzy rise in the flat Oxfordshire wheatlands the excitement all that summer had been intense. Up till that year nobody had given much thought to the Queen, and certainly she was hardly regarded with affection. She was held to be a tiresome old woman who had shut herself up in Balmoral Castle in widow's weeds and refused to open Parliament when Mr Gladstone had begged her to do so. Then suddenly opinion changed. She had reigned fifty years, and the newspapers were full of the achievements of her reign: railway travel, the telegraph, Free Trade, exports, progress, prosperity, Peace. "Fancy her reigning fifty years, the old dear, her," they said in the hamlet, and they bought paper flags to decorate their homes, and jam in glass jugs with her profile on them, and the women, poor as they were, subscribed a penny each (less than $\frac{1}{2}$p.) for a Jubilee present for the Queen, together with all the other women in England.

On Jubilee Day they were all up early. The mothers had to scrub the children from head to foot and put clean starched clothes on them, dispatch the men and the boys in their best Sunday suits to the farm where they were going to have a harvest home sort of dinner with sirloin of beef and Christmas pudding, and finally titivate themselves with all the carefully-hoarded finery that only came out very, very rarely. Then they ate a snack, but not so much as to take away their appetite for tea, and made their way to the park where they were going to be entertained.

A marquee had been set up, and here the villagers sat down to tea in relays, one parish at a time. There were clothes-baskets of bread and butter and jam, and watering cans of tea, already milked and sugared, and everybody ate hugely. Then after tea there were sports – races, grinning through a horse-collar to see who made the most grotesque face, climbing the greasy pole for a leg of mutton at the top. There were swings, roundabouts, and coconut shies too, and the local gentry moved among the throng, greeting them all but somehow rather quelling high spirits.

For Flora Timms the great experience of the day, beside which all the glories of Jubilee Day faded into insignificance, was seeing a girl no older than herself dance on a tightrope. She had paid a penny to go into the booth, and with a dozen or so others, stood in the sawdust watching the girl in her tinsel crown and tights, swaying gracefully along the rope stretched between two poles. To the country-bred Flora it was something utterly marvellous.

The Timms family were the first to return to the hamlet, but the merry-making was still going on in the park. They could see the trails of the rockets when they turned to look back, and the showers of golden rain above the dark trees. And, when they reached the garden gate the sound of the band playing God Save the Queen drifted through the air, and a roar of cheers.

Nothing ever seemed quite the same after the Jubilee, said Flora, writing fifty years later. The old rector died; the farmer for whom nearly every man in the hamlet worked had to make way for a gentleman farmer who brought with him new methods, including the self-binding reaping machine. It meant that women were no longer needed in the harvest field – a break with all the traditions of the past. "Several new brides took possession of houses previously

THE QUEEN PRESENTING JUBILEE MUGS

occupied by elderly people and brought new ideas into the place.
The last of the bustles disappeared, and leg-o'-mutton sleeves were
"all the go". The new rector's wife took her Mothers' Meeting for
a trip to London. Babies were christened new names; Wanda was
one, Gwendolen another. The innkeeper's wife got in cases of tinned
salmon and Australian rabbit. The Sanitary Inspector appeared
for the first time at the hamlet and shook his head over the pigsties
and privies. Wages rose, prices soared, and new needs multiplied.
People began to speak of 'before the Jubilee' – either as a golden
time or as one of exploded ideas, according to the age of the speaker."

And Flora, from 1939, looked back to the 1914–18 War, in which
her own brother was killed, and which in that peaceful Jubilee
decade was so entirely unforeseen.

"And all the time boys were being born or growing up in the
parish, expecting to follow the plough all their lives, or, at most to do

a little mild soldiering or go to work in a town. Gallipoli? Kut? Vimy Ridge? Ypres? What did they know of such places? But they were to know them, and when the time came they did not flinch. Eleven out of that tiny community never came back again. A brass plate on the wall of the church is engraved with their names. A double column, five names long, then, last and alone, the name of Edmund."

Russell

SINGING FOR THE QUEEN

"THE Queen is dead. Long live the King."

Russell Thorndike was fifteen when he heard his father make this announcement to parishioners at Rochester. "That sentence, echoed throughout the Empire, sounded like the death-knell of everything," he wrote in his account of the six years he had spent as a royal chorister. "England had grown used to the Queen for so long. The little figure of the great Widow of Windsor was a religious symbol. She stood for everything that Britons held sacred. And she was dead."

He felt it as a personal grief. As a Child of the Garter – a chorister of St George's Chapel, Windsor – he and his companions had sung for her many times. From the organ loft in the private chapel at Windsor Castle they could see her in the Royal Pew "so very close.

Being on the same level as ourselves she seemed to look us through and through, and we could distinctly hear her voice in the prayers and hymns. I can see the Queen now plainly, with her eyes on the preacher, nodding to herself when any point of his argument pleased her. Nothing escaped her. During the singing she kept an eye not only on us, but on her family too, in order to be sure that each voice was doing its best."

He had sung with the choir on many royal occasions. There were informal ones like birthday serenades; family services – the baptism and confirmation of royal grandchildren. There was the splendid affair of the Diamond Jubilee in 1897 when the boys had not only sung at a private service in St George's Chapel, but had seen her again two days later at the state Thanksgiving Service at St Paul's Cathedral. There had been funerals too when the Royal Vault had been used. He was a boy with a keen feeling for the past, and as he waited on a cold January night for the coffin of the Duke of Teck to be brought into the Chapel, "all the while I was thinking of those other Windsor boys who waited for the coffin of Charles the First. Just such a winter's night, and the Chapel very dark in the Nave, with a few dark shapes of Castle people still and silent."

He had friends in the Royal Household, and he had stayed with them at Osbourne and at Balmoral. He had travelled on the Royal Yacht and played with royal grandchildren. He was quite at home in Windsor Castle, and never nervous about singing for the Queen – for, as he reassured an eminent singer, "though the Queen had been a good vocalist in her youth and had sung before the great Mendelssohn, her singing days were passing, and most of us were better at it than she was." He loved royalty and state occasions and pageantry. He was impressed with the Kaiser Wilhelm II, not only because he understood music, but because he looked every inch an Emperor to Russell's eyes, and he treasured a little pebble connected with the first time he saw Wilhelm.

It was on the occasion of a state visit paid by Wilhelm to his grandmother, after the patching up of a quarrel between England and Germany. The cavalcade from the station to the Castle swept past the St George's boys, who were robed and standing just inside the Castle gates, ready to sing the German national anthem, and a stone dislodged by the Kaiser's carriage was flung up at Russell. He caught it and the Kaiser saw and laughed. "Even when the war caused his banner to be taken from the familiar stall in the Chapel,

"FROM MY HEART I THANK MY BELOVED PEOPLE. MAY GOD BLESS THEM. V.R. AND I."
THE QUEEN'S DIAMOND JUBILEE: HER MAJESTY TELEGRAPHING HER MESSAGE TO HER PEOPLE
THROUGHOUT THE EMPÍRE

I could never find it in my heart to throw away my stone, and I vowed that should I ever meet him on a battlefield I would present arms and sing 'Hear my Prayer'.* I wonder if he would have remembered."

He and the other boys at the school in the shadow of the Castle would cheer when on the Round Tower flagpost the Union Jack was struck, and the Royal Standard hoisted in its place. It meant

* Mendelssohn's famous anthem, apparently a great favourite with the Kaiser.

242

that Queen Victoria was in Windsor Castle. Though she rarely came to St George's Chapel itself, there was always the chance that you might be chosen to sing in her private chapel, and besides, the comings and goings and the activity when she was in residence were so exciting. The boys felt themselves a part of her household.

In a dilapidated book that had once been a stamp album, with dirty smudges of sticking paper on the pages to show where stamps had once been hinged, Russell kept a diary of his life at Windsor, and of the many public events in which he took part. There are also the letters he wrote home – very matter-of-fact, with much talk of food and long lists of royal personages and court officials whom he had seen at various functions; as a boy at a more ordinary school might have recorded the team at a house-match.

In this book appeared his account of the Queen's funeral, an occasion which he had thought was lost to him, as he was no longer a Child of the Garter; he had left the school a few weeks before.

The Queen died on 22 January, 1901 at Osborne, the house that she and the Prince Consort had built on the Isle of Wight. Russell felt it deeply; he was also bitterly disappointed that he was no longer among the choristers who would be singing for her for the last time. Two days later he was sitting gloomily at his new school listening to the headmaster telling him how foolish he had been to give so much time to music, so little to maths, when into the classroom came his father with a telegram. Russell was summoned to put on black clothes and join the senior members of the choir and Sir Walter Parratt* at Southampton, on their way to Osborne. "I walked out of that classroom," wrote the adult Russell, "feeling a great deal more important than when I went in."

A sense of importance surrounded him throughout the whole of the ensuing journey to Osborne. First there was the scurrying round to buy black trousers (they were never found; he had to wear striped ones), then the trip from Southampton in a special launch, and the sight of the Fleet at Cowes. They all stayed at the home of one of the choristers. "You could tell that only some great event could silence such a huge party," wrote the schoolboy Russell. "Everybody was solemn."

"After tea we drove up to Osborne House to sing at a service fixed

* Organist at St George's, Master of the Queen's Musick.

for six o'clock. When we first arrived we put on our surplices and waited in the Dining-room.

"Then we were ushered into the room where the Coffin lay in state. At one end was an Altar, but we could only look at the Coffin. It was guarded by four sentries of the Guards wearing their bearskins. There were four large candlesticks too. At the opposite end there were two pillars with a curtain and behind this we had to sing when the Royalty were assembled for these evening prayers.

"After the Service we waited a little, then the Chaplain asked leave if we might see the Coffin. He didn't know we had. What struck me first was the blazing little diamond crown that the Queen used to wear. It was placed on a cushion with the Queen's Order of the Garter, and her other orders. The blue ribbon of the Garter looked lovely. The Coffin was covered with her Majesty's Coronation Robes. A little crucifix of bronze with a silver figure of our Lord lay on the breast of the Coffin.

"At each corner of the Coffin a Grenadier Guard stood still with his rifle muzzle on the ground, keeping guard over the late Queen they had served.

"Next morning we walked down to Cowes. I felt rather above the other boys because I knew it all so well, and they had never seen it before, except of course Michael Smith who had lived there, and knew the Royalty like I did. Sir Walter was frightfully decent and gave us ten bob [50p.] to buy sweets with. Of course we didn't spend it all. We went on the parade instead of spending it all, and saw the battleships. We also saw a torpedo boat and a torpedo destroyer. Went home to dinner.

"After dinner we played with the pigs and gave each other rides in the donkey trap.

"Then we had tea, and thought once more about our business with the funeral. We went up to Osborne House again at the same time, but found that the service was at 6.30 instead of 6.00.

"After the service we were again permitted to see the Coffin, which to-night was covered with the cream pall which had been prepared for it. At each corner there was worked the Royal Arms. There was a large gold cross, worked into the cream pall, which gave it a very solemn appearance.

"The gold crown was placed on the cushion instead of the diamond one. The sceptre and the Orb insignia were placed at the foot of the

Coffin. Four Guards stood guard on each corner of the Coffin as on the previous evening.

"Then one of the servants who was kind of verger to the Sanctuary gave us each some flowers which had come off the Queen's Coffin. I got some lilies of the valley and some green. These I shall keep always, squashed.

"While walking a short cut across Osborne Grounds, we reached a shrubbery, and suddenly came upon some Horse Artillery practising with a gun-carriage and six horses, and on the gun-carriage was a lovely oak-and-brass-mounted coffin. They were rehearsing for the Funeral. We heard the leader say, 'We must try and go slower. We are going too fast.'

"It was not until this weird procession had passed into the darkness that I realized that Victoria the Great was dead."

Back at Windsor for the funeral they rehearsed the music, and then, on a bitterly cold January afternoon, waited in St George's chapel for the little coffin. It had been carried on the Royal Yacht from Osborne through a lane of battleships to Southampton. The funeral train had brought it to London; it had been borne through silent crowds to Paddington for its last journey to Windsor. But at Windsor where the Royal Horse Artillery were to take the coffin on the gun-carriage up the hill to St George's there was a sudden crisis; the horses, restive during the long wait in the bitter cold, had kicked over the traces. The Navy had come to the rescue; a team of sailors pulled the gun-carriage up the hill.

Waiting in the chapel, Russell was able to take in the scene: the press artists sketching up in the organ loft; the Lord Mayor of London and his Sheriffs; the gorgeously-robed Archbishops; the glitter of uniforms; the Lord Chief Justice in his huge wig and scarlet; Egyptians, Indians, Chinese; the reigning sovereigns of Europe. The choir stalls were filled with princes and ambassadors, and the choir had to stand by the altar, by the archbishops, and the kings who were the pall-bearers.

There was one last procession; the coffin was taken from Windsor across Windsor Great Park to be buried at Frogmore. The Moscow Bell, tolled only for the death of an English sovereign, sounded from the Round Tower; the massed bands of the Guards played the Chopin funeral march. The choristers stood round the sarcophagus and sang for the last time; the dust rattled on the coffin.

FUNERAL PROCESSION IN HIGH STREET, WINDSOR. SAILORS PULL THE GUN CARRIAGE UP TO THE CASTLE

"I have a treasure box in front of me," wrote the adult Russell Thorndike. "In it are my School badges. One, the Cross of St George; the other the crest of the Garter which St George's boys wear, instead of the cross, on caps and hats, when they have gained their double colours for games. Here is also the little pebble I have described which so amused the Kaiser. Also a small strip of purple felt which carpeted the floor and stands of St George's Chapel at the Queen's funeral. Also some pressed flowers which were given to me from the Queen's coffin at Osborne."

BIOGRAPHICAL NOTES AND SOURCES

SPANNING THE CENTURIES

For this chapter I have used Mary Howitt's *Autobiography* (1889), edited by her daughter Margaret, which also includes a chapter of reminiscences by William. I am also indebted to the biography of Mary and William: *Laurels and Rosemary* (Oxford University Press, 1955) by Amice Lee, herself a descendant of the family.

IN THE SHADOW OF THE FRENCH WARS

The material for this has been compiled from Mary Howitt's account of her childhood, *My Own Story* (1845), written for children, and from the autobiography above.

THE LITTLE FIFE-MAJOR

John Shipp (1784–1834) published his memoirs in 1829. They were frequently reprinted during the 19th century, sometimes in the form of a reward book for boys. He wrote a few other pieces, including two melodramas, and a pamphlet denouncing flogging.

THE POOR IRISH SCHOLAR

William Carleton, the Irish novelist, was born in 1794 and died in 1869. His unfinished autobiography was first published in 1896, and was reissued, edited by Patrick Kavanagh, in 1968 (MacGibbon & Kee). His *Traits and Stories of the Irish Peasantry* is largely founded on his own experiences; some, like *The Poor Scholar*, being directly autobiographical. Though he was born a Catholic he died a Protestant.

A HIGHLAND KINGDOM

Elizabeth Smith (born Elizabeth Grant) wrote her *Memoirs of a Highland Lady 1797–1830* for her children. She began them in 1845 and finished them in 1867. They were edited by her niece, Jane Maria Strachey, and published in 1898.

A ROMANTIC WANDERER

William Howitt's recollections of his youth are taken from the chapter in his wife's autobiography, mentioned above, and from *The Boy's Country Book* (1839).

THE RAGGED RADICAL WHO RAN AWAY

Alexander Somerville (1811–85) published his *Autobiography of a Working Man*, from which this chapter is taken, in 1848. It first appeared anonymously, as "by one who has whistled at the plough". He described his career as "persistently devoted to public well-being and to the removal of antagonism between extremes of society." He tried to earn a living by journalism, emigrated to Canada, and died in great want, in a shed in Toronto.

THE YOUNG NAVVY

The article on which this chapter is based appeared in *Household Words*, 21 June, 1856.

RIOTS AND THE WORKHOUSE

The articles by Charles Shaw from which this chapter is taken first appeared in the *Staffordshire Sentinel* between 1892 and 1893. They were published under the title *When I Was a Child* in 1903 and reissued in 1969 by S.R. Publishers.

THE SHIPWRECKED SHOEBLACK

His account of the wreck appeared in the *Ragged School Union Magazine*, April, 1854.

SETTLERS IN OHIO

The source for this chapter is *Our Cousins in Ohio* (1849).

COACHES AND RAILWAYS

The Rev. S. C. Scott (1838–1923), vicar of St John Baptist, Chester, wrote his memoirs *Things that Were* in 1923.

TWO MIDSHIPMEN AT SEBASTOPOL

R. E. B. Crompton, F.R.S. (1845–1940) was a pioneer of electrical engineering. His *Reminiscences*, which contain disappointingly little about his extraordinary boyhood experiences, were published in 1928.

Field Marshal Sir (Henry) Evelyn Wood, V.C. (1838–1919) wrote several books of military history, and published *From Midshipman to Field Marshal*, on which this account is based, in 1906.

GREAT EVENTS AT WINCHMORE HILL

This chapter is drawn entirely from the little booklet *Winchmore Hill, Memories of a Lost Village* (1912) in the British Museum. The Enfield Public Libraries also possess a copy. It is apparently all that Miss Cresswell ever wrote.

THE LORD LIEUTENANT'S SON

Frederic Hamilton (1856–1928) spent many years in the Diplomatic Service. He and his brother Ernest were indefatigable writers of memories of Victorian days. This chapter is taken from *The Days Before Yesterday* (1920), by courtesy of Hodder and Stoughton, and Doubleday and Co. Inc.

THE MODERN GIRL

Elizabeth Grant's memoirs and Mary Howitt's Autobiography have already been mentioned. M. Vivian Hughes (this was Molly Thomas's married name) wrote three volumes of reminiscences, from the second of which, *A London Girl of the Eighties*, I have taken much of the material for this chapter. They were published in a single volume as *A London Family 1870–1900* by the Oxford University Press in 1946.

JUBILATION DAY

Ernest Shepard, famous for his illustrations, particularly to A. A. Milne, wrote and illustrated an account of his childhood which he called *Drawn from Memory*. It was published in 1957 by Methuen and Co. and by J. B. Lippincott Co., by whose courtesy these extracts are printed.

Flora Thompson's accounts of Oxfordshire in the 1880's and '90's were collected under the title *Lark Rise to Candleford*, and published by the Oxford University Press in 1945.

SINGING FOR THE QUEEN

Russell Thorndike (1885–1973), actor and writer, brother of Dame Sybil Thorndike, wrote about his experiences as a Windsor chorister in *Children of the Garter* (1937). The extracts from this book are reproduced by courtesy of the Hutchinson Publishing Group.

THE ILLUSTRATIONS

I have used the abbreviation I.L.N. for the Illustrated London News. J.J. is used for illustrations taken from the John Johnson Collection in the Bodleian Library, Oxford, and V. & A. Lib. indicates that the book in question is in the collection of children's books in the Victoria & Albert Museum Library, London. Unless specifically stated, all other illustrations have been photographed from books in the Bodleian, or in my own possession.

49 William Carleton's birthplace. Carleton: *Traits and Stories of the Irish Peasantry* (1843).

51 Boys playing with a toy cannon. William Howitt: *The Boy's Country Book* (1839).

53 Ribbonmen swearing their oath on the altar. From Carleton as above.

55 A hedge school. From Carleton as above.

57 From Carleton as above.

59 An outdoor altar. From Carleton as above.

61 A ferryboat. From *Rural Scenes*. As p. 25.

63 David Allan: The 4th Duke of Atholl and his family. By courtesy of the Duke of Atholl, Blair Atholl, Perthshire.

64 Drawing by an unknown artist of a ballroom scene, c. 1810. J.J.

67 Highland piper. From W. H. Pyne: *The Costume of Great Britain* (1808).

69 Highland shepherd. As above.

73 David Allan: *The Penny Wedding*. This probably shows a Lowland rather than a Highland scene. The National Galleries of Scotland, Edinburgh.

74 Engraving after G. Jones, dated 1822. J.J.

76 The timber carriage. From *Rural Scenes*. As p. 25.

78, 79 From William Howitt: *The Boy's Country Book* (1839).

81 Paying the due at the tollgate; a scene that William Howitt must often have encountered. Engraving after R. Cooper. J.J.

84 Newstead Abbey, 1834. Etching after M. Webster. Nottingham Public Libraries.

86 The collier. From George Walker: *The Costume of Yorkshire in 1814*.

88 Loading a collier at Newcastle-on-Tyne. From Isaac Taylor: *The Mine* (1845).

90 The shepherd. From *Rural Scenes*. As p. 25.

91 From W. H. Pyne: *On Rustic Figures* (1817).

93 Alexander Carse: *Cottage Interior*. The National Galleries of Scotland, Edinburgh.

95 George Harvey: *The Village School*, 1826. Obviously a much milder schoolmaster than the one described. The National Galleries of Scotland, Edinburgh.

97 The harvest home, and oxen and cart. From *Rural Scenes*. As p. 25.

101 From W. H. Pyne: *On Rustic Figures* (1817).

102 Alexander Carse: *The Cottar's Saturday Night*. These cottagers, seen at evening prayers, lived in greater comfort than the Somervilles, but shared the same piety. The National Galleries of Scotland, Edinburgh.

104 From *Railway Alphabet*. As p. 20.

106 Titlepage of a children's book of 1883. Mrs Garnett did much missionary work among the navvies in the 1870's and '80's. Her name is spelt wrongly on the book.

108 Working shaft, Kilsby tunnel. From J. C. Bourne: *London to Birmingham Railway* (1839). This is the line that "Dandy Dick" worked on.

111 Watford tunnel face. As above.

113 *Railway Alphabet*. As p. 20.

115 Making the embankment at Wolverton Valley. From J. C. Bourne. As p. 108.

116 *Railway Alphabet*. As p. 20.

117 Factory children. Detail from George Walker: *The Costume of Yorkshire in 1814*.

119 I.L.N. (1842).

122 A dame school. From a scrapbook in the Print Room, Victoria and Albert Museum.

123 The potter and his mould runner. From W. H. Pyne: *The Costume of Great Britain* (1808).

125 Staffordshire. Page from *Reuben Ramble's Travels* (c. 1850). V. & A. Lib.

127 "In search of a suburban famine house." *Pictorial Times*, c. 1844. J.J.

129 "Poor Law imprisonment." As above.

132 Emigrants' arrival at Cork. I.L.N. (1850).

134 The departure. As above.

136 Between decks on an emigrant ship. As above.

137 Wreck of the Burhampooter off Margate. I.L.N. (1843).

138 Carrying the emigrants from the wreck. As above.

140 The settlers' wagon. From Edward King: *The Southern States of North America* (1875).

142 "The 'John Ross house' near Chattanooga." As above.

143 Settlement of Nashoba. From Frances Trollope: *Domestic Manners of the Americans* (1832).

144 An old negro herb doctor. As p. 140.

145 A negro prayer meeting. As p. 140.

146 A negro cabin on the banks of the Tennessee. As p. 140.

148 "A future politician." As p. 140.

149 Thrashing walnuts. From *Rural Scenes*. As p. 25.

152 Attack on a potato store by starving Irish. I.L.N. (1842).

153 The well. From *Rural Scenes*. As p. 25.

154 Nutting. From *Rural Scenes*. As p. 25.

155 Gathering apples. From *Rural Scenes*. As p. 25.

157 The Christmas tree. From Mrs Valentine: *Games for Family Parties* (c. 1860).

159 *The Alphabet of Nations*. As p. 48.

160 Monument Bridge Hull, 1840. This is the view that the Scott boys would have seen from their nursery window when Samuel was two years old. From an engraving by P. Brannon in the Kingston-upon-Hull Museum.

161 Wharf. From *City Scenes*. As p. 24.

165 The mail change. One of a series of prints published by A. Park. J.J.

166 Early Victorian mail coach. J.J.

167 The opening of the railway at Swansea. I.L.N., J.J.

168 Early rolling stock. J.J.

170 Title page of children's book of 1851.

171 "The Shilling Day." I.L.N. (1851).

173 "Remonstrance." Drawing by John Leech: *Pictures of Life and Character* (1863).

176 Volunteer review, Hyde Park, 1860. I.L.N. (1860).

177 Midshipmen's quarters, 1817. J.J.

183 The sailors' battery before Sebastopol. I.L.N. (1855).

184 Ambulance transport. I.L.N. (1855).

186 Assault on the Redan. I.L.N. (1855).

189 The sick deck on the Belleisle hospital ship. I.L.N. (1855). .

192 Bicycle manufacturers' catalogue. This does not show the sort of velocipede described on p. 197, but the "boneshaker" introduced about 1865. J.J.

195 J.J.

196 "Photographic Beauties." Drawing by John Leech. As p. 173.

198 Social tricycle. This is not the model described in the text, which appears to have been an experimental model. From a Christmas card. J.J.

200 Boxmoor embankment. From J. C. Bourne. As p. 108.

201 The viaduct, Folkestone. From an engraving by J. Saddler, c. 1850. J.J.

202 Winchmore Hill Station, c. 1890. From a photograph in the London Borough of Enfield Public Libraries.

204 Two pages, one of whom is probably Frederic Hamilton, in ceremonial dress. Detail from p. 212.

207 The railway disaster described in the text. I.L.N. (1868).

209 Reception of the Lord Lieutenant at Dublin. Not, unfortunately, the Duke of Abercorn himself, but his successor. I.L.N. (1869).

212 Installation of the Prince of Wales as a Knight of St Patrick. I.L.N. (1867).

214 Firing at the Fenians at Tallagh. I.L.N. (1867).

215 Nobility driving to a royal "drawing-room". From *City Scenes*. As p. 24.

216 *Girl's Own Paper* (1882).

218 Four pages from W. Upton: *The School-Girl in 1820* (William Darton, 1820). From the Osborne Collection of Early Children's Books, Toronto Public Library.

220 I.L.N. (1879).

223 *Girl's Own Paper* (1882).

227 *Girl's Own Paper* (1882).

229 From the supplement to *The Queen*, 18 June, 1887. J.J.

232 J.J.

235 I.L.N. (1887).

238 Florence Dunn receives a Jubilee mug for her record of unbroken attendance at school from the age of five to twelve. I.L.N. (1887).

240 Children and former royal servants bring funeral wreaths to St George's Chapel, Windsor. I.L.N. (1901).

242 The Queen sending a Diamond Jubilee message by telegraph. "From my heart I thank my beloved people. May God bless them. V.R. and I." I.L.N. (1897).

246 Funeral procession. I.L.N. (1901).

INDEX